I0814932

THE GREEN~WOOD CARVER

THE GREEN~WOOD CARVER

SLOW WOODCRAFT FOR BEGINNERS

Samuel Alexander

Skittledog

Contents

The healing power of woodcraft

I began carving as a response to a rough patch in my life but my journey soon became a beautiful discovery of how craft can help people like me to centre themselves. I knew that from my first push of the knife into wood that I had unveiled something truly healing. It was as if the slow, spiralling shavings of wood were pirouetting away my troubles and transporting me into a calm, harmonious state, like a walk through a forest. It found me when I was weighed down by a dark cloud of depression and provided a place where I could channel my energy and express myself. Craft set the foundations of my recovery and taught me how to develop creative methods of understanding my thoughts.

While you are carving, you have the opportunity to look within, slow down and to process things. I like to think of each piece I make as a poem, written in wood, each facet expressing an emotion and mood. Time is locked into the wood you carve, stamped within the grain and growth rings. A deep heritage of carving techniques connect us to generations of committed makers. Each handmade piece is a celebration of the natural world and human creativity and immersing myself in this heritage has given me a holistic view of what it truly means to be present.

Freshly felled, green wood, with its high moisture content, naturally lends itself to working with hand tools and gives a distinct and intuitive carving experience, bringing us closer to nature and asking less of the body than dry, seasoned timber. Starting from a humble log, working in green wood is a sustainable organic process without any external intervention apart from the growth of the tree itself. The unpredictability of wood often conjures up unique characteristics – even the act of splitting a log opens a new conversation, a collaboration full of surprising possibilities. As we work the wood, we respond to it, make decisions, even compromise, choosing to retain, rework, or simply leave things behind.

Simple beginnings

With the earliest known carvings made over 12,000 years ago, creative woodcraft is deeply rooted within our ancestral history. In fact, you could say that the foundations of our human existence were formed by a strong relationship with wood. It was our source of heat, formed our settlements, provided tools and utensils and was important for worship, storytelling, travel, art and sculpture. Not only has our world been hewn from these primitive preliminaries, but the sensory feeling of working with wood is an instinctive echo that connects us to the past. The excitement of cracking open a log, the visceral sound of the fibres splintering and the sweet aroma that swirls through the nose must have been vividly experienced by our ancestors.

Woodcarving is a release of energy, both positive and negative, channelled and documented into tangible objects.

Although the act of carving has shifted in significance since our early years of human survival, there is no denying the vital bond with nature and consciousness that woodcraft can nurture. Our dependency on technology, mass production and the screen has clouded our connection to the natural and tangible world – and while it may seem as though we no longer require wood to survive, the drifting instinct towards the simple form of carving may suggest otherwise.

I believe the craft universe is growing, allowing us to gain artistic and cognitive skills that not only provide a healing, meditative environment but also allow us to achieve rewarding and tactile results. In this universe, carving green wood will no doubt thrive as a therapeutic vocation, capable of contributing greatly to our positive wellbeing and increasing our understanding and respect for the natural world around us.

The modern green-wood carver requires just three modest tools: an axe, carving knife and hook knife (see page 28). The age-old techniques remain slow and clear for all to pick up. There have been many woodcarving movements over history but none feel as accessible as the version we see today.

The vast carving community is diverse, generous and connected through workshops and festivals spread across the world that all celebrate green woodworking. After feeling isolated for years, I felt guided by this comforting craft to reach out to other makers and set foot into this extremely welcoming family of like-minded folk. I soon joined a small woodcarving cooperative in London, which became a sanctuary that nourished my skills and friendships.

After attending a talk promoting social prescription within communities, I saw that my skills and learning could be shared to benefit others. I set out to create a ripple, hopeful that, with craft, I could reach those who may need it. I developed an affordable course that has taught over a thousand people how to carve a wooden spoon from a log with hand tools. Each wood chip that fell to the ground contributed to a thick carpet that quilted the workshop.

As I had hoped, a pattern slowly surfaced where participants were attending the course to centre themselves as a response to their own complex obstacles. For some, each wood chip signified letting go; for others, each facet allowed them to gain something they lacked. Many participants have continued to make – some now make professionally, while others host their own classes.

With this book, I hope to increase that ripple I started many years ago. With tips and notes on preparation, tools, wood and step-by-step instructions for a range of beautiful handmade projects, it is meant to offer a starting point, one to ignite your mindful woodcarving journey. It is the book I wish I'd had when I first began carving and I hope it connects you closely to the sensory joy of craft and gives a deep understanding of what it truly means to make.

Preparing to carve

Wood is a mystical material full of unique quirks and properties and requires sensitivity and patience to work and carve. This section explains how to understand the wood you are about to work with and how to prepare yourself and your tools before you start.

Wonderful wood

Trees are comforting spectators of our human existence, documenting their whole life with an album of stamped growth rings like annual self-portraits. Similar to trees, we grow uniquely; we are upright, with limbs, we have funny crown-like hair and we are incredibly diverse. We also reproduce, we breathe, we communicate with others, we protect ourselves from changes, we remember and we die. Yet, when it comes to our leafy friends, there is still so much we do not know.

Getting to know trees

Some basic knowledge of trees in the form of simple identification can help contribute to a greater universal understanding and respect for them. Though there are thousands upon thousands of different tree species out there, leaning to identify them doesn't have to be daunting – in fact, it can be quite fun. Trees are categorized and identified by characteristics such as their ability to lose their leaves in winter, their bark colour and texture, crown shape, leaf shape and structure, flowers, fruits, twigs and buds. The more tree varieties you meet, the easier it gets and the more confident you become – I once met a chap who could successfully identify most green woods from a log pile with his sense of smell.

There are now many user-friendly tree identification resources, making access to today's tree knowledge even more available and digestible. When starting a tree ID journey, with a tree guide, try taking some familiar walks where you will encounter previously overlooked trees, or use a well-reviewed tree identification app to add some expertise. Tree identification courses in the form of informative tree walks are growing increasingly popular. They are an illuminating and wholesome way of connecting with trees, outside spaces and with other aspiring tree enthusiasts.

Sourcing green wood

It can sometimes be tricky to get your hands on fresh green wood for carving – there is an element of patience, and maybe some networking needed, but once wood comes your way, it is extremely rewarding and you will likely have met some new friends along the way.

Reaching out

Firstly, as the popularity of green woodworking is growing widely, ask around your local area to see if there are makers nearby; I like to think that you are never too far away from another carver who might be able to help by sharing some of their own wood or contacts. Try reaching out to similar organizations such as local Forest School clubs or community workshops to see if there are any other makers or carving groups nearby. From experience, I have noticed there are often established groups of green woodworkers in larger cities or urban environments that are more than happy to share their know-how.

On a forest floor, wood quickly becomes home to wildlife, contributing to a woodland's incredible biodiversity. Be mindful not to disrupt habitats if there are signs of life and only take what you need.

It may also be worth politely reaching out to local arborists, park wardens, landscaping companies or your local council to see if they have any plans to fell a tree in your area and ask if they might be happy to share the wood. Don't be disheartened if they either don't reply or turn you away – they are usually busy people, with a predetermined plan that involves the deposit of the wood or chippings. Sadly, many trees are felled because they are diseased and so professionals will have a plan to responsibly dispose of infected green waste to stop the spread to other trees or vegetation.

Explore on foot

Often, just by taking a walk through a local public woodland you may find some suitable wood on the ground, though be mindful of how long this wood may have been sat for, since sometimes it can rot and be too brittle or crumbly to work with. Sometimes storms can bring down trees in local woodland so be cautious straight after a storm. Allow plenty of time for any overhead branches to fall from canopies.

The sound of a chainsaw on the horizon can be a very promising start. If you have time, scout out the source of the sound and what is being felled. Never jump a cordoned-off area to get the tree surgeon's attention; always wait for a good time or a break in their work before inquiring. Often, a friendly tree surgeon will be interested in your journey and be happy for you to take a log or two to carve at home. It's also worth asking what the tree surgeons tend to do with their logs – some throw them in the chipper and sell/donate as mulch and others deposit logs at a lumber yard that may sell them.

Selecting wood for carving

Some woods display particular characteristics that make them preferred over others but ideally, you want to be carving deciduous, hardwood trees rather than softwood.

Hardwoods

These are fairly easy to identify because they tend to shed their leaves in winter. The grain structure of hardwood is often tighter, more stable and reliable for carving and is also stronger compared to more fibrous softwoods.

There are many different hardwoods to explore and you will discover your own favourites. Fruit woods, such as cherry, plum and apple, are beautiful in tone and colour and dramatic in grain patterns but they are usually denser and harder to carve than other woods such as lime, birch or alder. Although these may not be as characterful, they are less compact, less demanding and are perfect learning material.

Sycamore (maple) and beech are reliable, versatile woods that usually grow straight and have an interlocked flecked structure that shimmers when held to light, revealing their medullary rays. Sycamore smells like freshly chopped cucumber when split open and beech typically warps as it dries.

Some woods are susceptible to spalting – fungal decay that casts unique colourings. If spalting is caught at the right time in woods like maple, beech or birch, it can leave behind dramatic patterns. If left too long, it will begin to weaken and rot the log, making it unusable. Yew and laburnum are thought to be toxic so work them with caution and avoid for food use.

Anatomy of a log

Pith The origin of the tree, containing the stem from when the tree was a sapling.
Heartwood Harder timber, often darker in colour.
Sapwood Lighter, softer and younger wood.
Cambium Aids wood and bark cell growth.
Bark The wood's armour against predators and changes to moisture.

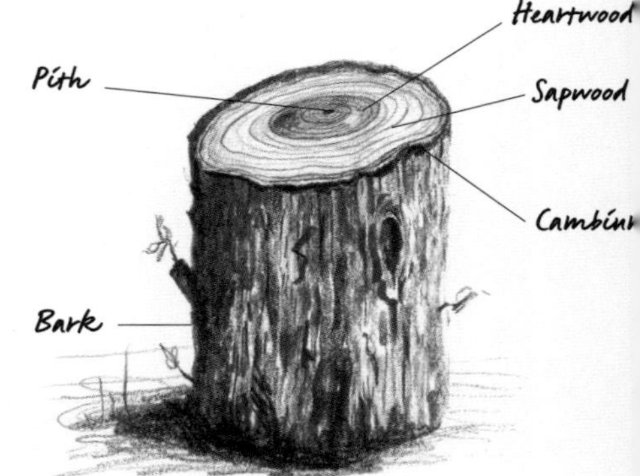

Timber inspection

When selecting a log, check the surface of the bark and inspect for small holes that suggest the wood has been occupied by woodworm or grubs. These holes may interfere with the structural integrity of the object you make. Cracks or crumbly, rotten wood on the end grain indicate that the wood may be too far gone and has succumbed to the elements. The bark will also suggest how knotty or twisted the grain of the wood is. Though these features can be interesting to incorporate, the unpredictability can often cause challenges.

Retaining moisture

Unless you can carve it right away, keep the moisture content in the wood high until it is time to carve. The log can be covered in a damp cloth for a short time but if you can't carve it for a week or two, seal each end of the round with a coat of wood glue (or PVA) and cover with a tarp on the ground. If you can't carve for a month or so, and have a large enough freezer, you can seal the log in a bag or plastic wrap and freeze. You can also pre-split the log into smaller sections before sealing. Larger logs will thaw naturally over a few hours and smaller billets can be run under a tap to break down the ice.

Prepare your space and yourself

Before starting to carve, I like to lay the groundwork. I ready myself and my surroundings so I can feel trust. Knowing my needs are met means I can confidently enter into a safe and relaxing woodcarving state.

Your carving space

Creating a safe and comfortable habitat to carve in can actually be quite an indulgent thing to do. I love working outside where I can. A simple outdoor garden set-up does not need to be complex. A stump of wood to chop at and a comfortable place to sit, ideally with the option of some shelter, is all that is needed.

Carving can be messy, and inviting it into the home comes with its disadvantages – usually in the form of dispersing wood chips everywhere. They can easily be caught in an open bedsheet with weights on each corner.

Things to consider:

Light Good lighting is important for safety. Natural light is best, but strong, high-contrast lighting is very useful to see any mistakes or unwanted textures on your carving.

Space Give yourself enough space to comfortably sit and carve without knocking your elbows on tables, walls or other people. Keep everything at least at an arm's length.

Distractions It's a nice feeling to be carving knowing you're not going to be suddenly surprised or interrupted. Let others know what you're up to and where you will be.

Clothing I recommend comfortable clothes, not your best ones, and closed-toe shoes too – just in case.

Mindful preparation

When you are experiencing new crafts, a new and shiny creative tap is opened. However, the tap needs time for the sludgy water to run through first, before you get to the clear stuff. Be realistic with your outcomes when you're learning and be mindful that your first ten or so wooden spoons might not look like the ones you have seen by the experienced makers when scrolling through your Instagram feed. Here are some tips to create space for healthy learning habits.

Ground yourself
Bring your awareness to your feet, feeling the ground underneath you. Then feel the weight of your body and the gravity that is pulling you down. How does your body feel today? Inhale slowly, filling your lungs, feeling the air expanding your whole chest. Notice something that is present in your space, your body and your mind. Exhale slowly, gently and fully, visualizing air travelling out of your body, your chest falling back down. Here is an opportunity to consciously let go of what does not serve you now.

Allow time
Carving is a slow and laborious craft that requires patience. Your outcome will not benefit from being rushed. You will be at greater risk of cutting yourself when using tools in a more frantic manner.

Take breaks
When carving, you are constantly making decisions of 'yes or no': should a piece of wood stay on my project, yes or no? Although these questions may seem rather simple to answer, they sometimes aren't and they can lead to decision fatigue and a lack of focus. You will find that coming back to your project with a fresh pair of eyes and stretched, relaxed muscles will offer more clarity. Taking a 20–30 minute break for every two hours of carving will help.

A moment to stretch

Although woodcarving is capable of mindfully easing many of life's troubles, practising repetitive motions while engaging unused muscle groups for long periods of time could trigger other unwanted issues. Taking just a few moments to stretch can go a long way to increase strength and mobility and prevent injuries. Try this short routine before, during breaks and after carving, repeating twice each time.

Shoulders/triceps

Stand tall and slowly roll your neck around. Circle the shoulders backwards, focusing on the opening of the chest and the mobility of the shoulders. Repeat a few times, then touch hands behind the back with one arm up and over the shoulder and the other under. Hold for 10 seconds and then switch hands. Bring one arm across the chest and hold with the other arm at the elbow for the same amount of time – switch and repeat.

Forearms

Interlock your fingers and touch the elbows together. Slowly create a figure of eight in a relaxed motion with the wrists. Next, move into a prayer stretch by bringing both palms together, into the chest. Raise the elbows out as if to pray until the stretch is felt. Next, raise the dominant arm straight out in front, with the palm facing the floor. Gently pull the dominant hand back towards the body to feel the stretch in the forearm, holding for 10 seconds. Repeat the same motion with the palm up. Switch arms and repeat.

Hands

Open the hands and stretch each finger apart as wide as possible and hold for 20 seconds. Squeeze the thumb in a closed fist and pivot your hand away until you feel the stretch and hold. Lastly, pull each individual finger backwards gently to feel the stretch, holding for 2–3 seconds each.

Build your stamina

It may be some time before you can carve for hours on end. You will likely build blisters and develop cramps if you have been carving for too long. Generally, if you are asking yourself if it is time to stop for the day, the answer is yes.

Tools for green woodcarving

These are the three most important tools required to begin your green woodcarving journey.

Carving axe

The axe is an unforgivingly beautiful tool. It is big, sharp and often misunderstood as being unsafe. Axe confidence takes time to build but I regard it as the most balanced and safest of the three main tools. A carving axe is usually the first tool used on a project, typically removing up to 90 per cent of the waste material. It is likely to have a slightly bowed handle and a curved cutting edge on a weighty head to encourage an accurate slice through the wood fibres.

Carving knife

The carving knife is capable of implementing as much expression as a paintbrush. It manoeuvres in various ways depending on the style of the cut. It can boldly cut large facets, peel away shavings with precision and intent or nimbly graze the surface with meticulous refinement. I recommend a fixed-blade carving knife rather than a folding knife or a pocket knife. Carbon steel is preferable over mild or stainless steel since it is much more reliable and easier to maintain.

Hook knife

A hook knife (sometimes known as a spoon knife) is a curved, 'U' shaped piece of steel with a cutting edge on one side. It is a unique tool. Unlike a carving knife that slices and glides, the hook knife sweeps shavings away to hollow and create concave forms. It is mostly used to efficiently excavate the bowl of a wooden spoon.

J.Wood

Other useful tools and materials

Axe block

You will need an axe block – a big, lumpy round of wood with a width of around 30cm (12in), used as a chopping surface to support the wood at different angles and absorb the blows from the axe without damaging the sharp edge. The axe block can be situated on the ground, used in a seated position to one side of the body, or be elevated by three splayed legs to use while standing. This increases safety and encourages better posture (see page 44).

Saw

A general-use hand saw will gradually make its way through a log, but the larger teeth, wide frame and rigidity of a bow saw will make for a much easier cut. Pruning saws, designed to tear through green branches, cut on the pull with ease and come in an array of sizes. I also recommend a small Nokogiri or Japanese saw to accurately remove small sections of wood.

Heavy wooden club or mallet

For splitting wood – this can be a log, tapered into a handle, or a weighty branch.

A pencil or two

Anything softer than 2B is ideal for drawing on wet wood. Pens are not recommended as the ink can bleed into the wood fibres.

Drill and drill bits

I prefer a hand-powered drill, but the electric one is admittedly easier. Don't forget a broad range of wood-specific drill bits.

Bench vice

This allows you to have both hands free when sawing or drilling. Alternatively, use a 'C' clamp on the end of the table, or even a bench hook. (Place a thin piece of wood between the vice and the surface before applying pressure to avoid marking it.)

Measuring devices

A simple ruler or tape measure will be useful.

First aid

Have a suitable first aid kit in reaching distance, containing ample amounts of bandages of different shapes and sizes (the long wrapping finger strips are very useful), some sterilizing wound wipes, plenty of gauze and tape and some steri-strips. A tourniquet and the knowledge of how to use one is strongly recommended. It is also useful to have some clean, absorbent cloth nearby that can be applied to a wound to add pressure quickly.

If you have cut yourself, quickly apply pressure directly onto the cut using a clean bandage or tea towel. Press down firmly and, if possible, bring it to a level above your heart. Keep applying pressure for up to 10 minutes. Once it has stopped, use either clean running water or a sterilized wound wipe to clean, and dress appropriately, re-dressing when required.

Go immediately to your nearest emergency department if your wound looks to be deep and/or long, does not stop bleeding or if the blood comes out in spurts. Between your legs, in your groin area, the femoral artery transports blood to your legs and lies approximately half an inch below the surface. When carving, always keep the knife away from the inside of your legs to prevent a serious cut to this area.

Carving safely

Woodcarving tools are to be deeply respected. Even the most experienced of woodcarvers encounter accidents from time to time, but most happen when first learning how to use hand tools. Here are some simple habits that go a long way to protect yourself, and others.

Don't carve alone

It's good practice not to carve without other people nearby in case of emergencies, when you may need another pair of hands or eyes.

Sheath your tools

An unaccompanied, exposed blade in any workshop setting is a recipe for disaster. Whenever you stop carving, make it a habit to keep your tool sheathed. When unsheathing, do keep your sheath in a handy pocket that is quick and easy to access.

Maintain tool sharpness

Blunt tools cause more accidents as they require more force to drive through wood. This creates a higher risk of a dangerous slip. A sharp knife will glide through wood with less force and more control, meaning that it is much easier to stop.

Transporting tools

I wouldn't recommend transporting your tools unless you really need to – for example, if you're going to a workshop or carving event. If you are transporting your tools, tape the sheaths shut while in transit.

Keep a clear head

Sharp tools shouldn't be used if alcohol or mind-altering substances have been consumed. If you are taking prescribed medication that makes you drowsy, consult with your doctor before carving.

Sharpening your tools

Sharp tools contribute to a positive woodcarving experience, requiring much less force, making them more obedient and, as a result, considerably safer. A knife that doesn't have to struggle through wood will leave behind a more polished finish where the edge has passed with little disruption.

Sharpening is an acquired skill of many methods and preferences that all take time to fully grasp and understand. It's useful to think of sharpening as flattening – imagine if you observe the edge of a blunt carving knife under a microscope, it will be slightly rounded where it will have repeatedly penetrated wood fibres. Sharpening is a restoration of this edge using a graduation of abrasives from coarse to fine. Minuscule amounts of metal are removed from both sides of the bevel to re-establish the point, while maintaining its determined angle (20–25° for knives and 30° for axes). All carving knives and most axe bevels are ground into a centred point. Some axes are ground in favour of one bevel to aid someone who is right- or left-handed.

The bevel

A bevel is the section of the metal that has been ground away into a point to form the edge. Woodcarving tool edges are ground to specific angles and lengths that are pivotal in the efficient removal of wood. An angle too great would require far too much force and precarious energy to drive through wood fibres cleanly. On the other hand, an angle too acute and long would likely roll and fold and will never retain its sharpness.

Home sharpening set-up

Using abrasive wet and dry sandpaper for sharpening is simple and inexpensive. The sheets of paper come in a variety of grits that effectively remove varying amounts of metal depending on the severity of the blunt tool. A 120 grit will re-establish the bevel of a sad-looking knife and 600 will provide the perfect starting point to revive a slightly dull edge. By taping each end of the paper sheets onto a small, flat raised platform, you essentially make a series of whetstones that can be applied to all three tools. The abrasives will slowly remove metal and brush it towards the cutting edge, raising a small, hair-like piece of steel (sometimes invisible to the eye) called a burr. The grits are worked up, graduating to a slightly finer one each time to hone the scratch pattern. The burr can be removed with a final pass against a leather strop: a suede side-up piece of leather or leather alternative, conditioned with a sharpening compound, glued to a flat surface.

I have seen tools that have lasted decades, passed through generations, still sharp and carving admirably.

Materials for sharpening

- Table or surface to work at
- Packet of wet and dry sandpaper sheets with frequent grit intervals of 120–3000 grit
- Non-slip mat
- Small, flat platform such as a tile, flat piece of wood board or glass
- Parcel/masking tape
- Piece of dowel, smaller than the diameter of the curvature of your hook knife
- Marker pen
- Leather strop and compound

Sharpening a carving knife

Tape each end of the abrasive sheet to the tile or board, ensuring that the paper is taut and flat, with a long edge meeting the lip of the elevated surface. Place the elevated abrasive surface onto the non-slip mat.

1. Colour the bevel on each side of the carving knife blade with the marker pen. The knife is going to be brushed away from the direction of the cutting edge with the bevel in constant contact with the abrasive. Colouring each bevel will reveal where it is successfully in contact, and where the brushing pattern misses.

2. With the handle in your dominant hand, rest the knife on the flat surface with the edge directed away and find the flat spot of the bevel by rocking the knife into the abrasive. Once you have found the flat spot, place your index, middle and ring fingers along the length of the opposite bevel to steady the knife and brush or drag it away from the edge. Try to engage less of your wrist and more of the elbows and shoulders when pushing, minimizing any unwanted rotation that may lead to accidental rounding and convexing of the bevels.

3. Study the marker pen wear to see if the contact against the abrasive was well distributed across the bevel. To sharpen towards the tip, press with your ring finger into the bevel and raise the handle slightly when sharpening. This can be tricky to master at the beginning because all knife shapes are different. Firstly, try pushing the blade into the abrasive without brushing it to feel how much the knife handle needs to rise to engage the tip before pushing or pulling to establish the angle.

4. Once you have successfully removed the pen marks from both bevels, replace the abrasive with a finer grit and repeat, graduating with frequent intervals up to a grit of at least 3000. Lastly, to remove any burr from the edge, make a final pass or two against the leather strop for a razor-sharp finish.

Sharpening an axe

The set-up for the axe is the same as the knife – reuse the same starting abrasive, taped to the flat surface, and the bevel edges highlighted with the marker pen.

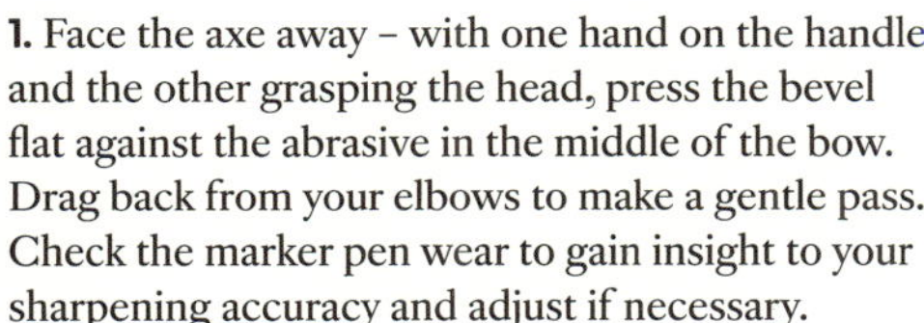

1. Face the axe away – with one hand on the handle and the other grasping the head, press the bevel flat against the abrasive in the middle of the bow. Drag back from your elbows to make a gentle pass. Check the marker pen wear to gain insight to your sharpening accuracy and adjust if necessary.

2. To sharpen the whole length, gently drop or raise the axe handle, steering it slightly to the left or right while pressing the bevel into the abrasive. Work from the middle to the toe and heel to remove the marker pen and the metal, pushing a burr to the edge. Repeat for both sides, swapping hands. Work up the grits in frequent intervals to around 3000 for a mirror finish and make a final few passes on the leather strop to remove any remaining burr.

Sharpening a hook knife

The hook knife is the most difficult to sharpen. The bevel that runs on the inside of the curve is flat and the outer edge is either convex or ground at an angle to form the edge. When sharpening, the main focus is on the flat bevel on the inside of the curve. To successfully remove metal here, keep the knife still and use the dowel with the abrasive wrapped around to brush the inner bevel.

1. Highlight the bevels on both the inside of the curve and the outside with the marker pen.

2. Wrap the starting abrasive around the dowel, pulling it tight with no bumps. Hold the handle firmly in your non-dominant hand, with the curvature of the hook facing upwards with the knife resting on the non-slip mat.

3. In your dominant hand, rock the dowel from the spine onto the bevel slowly to connect with the flat surface. Placing your index finger onto the back of the dowel will give you greater control and tension. Push the dowel away from the cutting edge, making good use of the whole length of the abrasive, and begin lifting the knife handle to work down towards the tight curve of the blade. Be mindful of the location of your index finger when pushing the dowel towards the edge.

4. For the back bevel, revert back to the flat surface with the matching grit taped to it, swapping hands to hold the handle in your dominant hand while supporting the knife with your non-dominant fingers on the inside bevel, being mindful to distance them from the cutting edge. Guide the knife away slowly, ensuring that your dominant hand is the one to push the blade away while your other hand is only providing stability.

5. Repeat with frequent changes up the grits to around 3000, with a final pass against the strop on the outside edge.

Little and often

The key to maintaining the edge of a tool is to routinely practise sharpening before the edge reveals its bluntness. A 'little and often' habitual approach with the last two finishing grits and the strop, whenever picking up your knife, will save hours of sharpening. Protect your knives from materials and substances that may decay or chip away at their edge by keeping them dry and sheathed when not carving.

Building your skills

Learning some key techniques will set a strong, confident foundation to grow and progress. By taking time to practise with your tools, you can nip any unsafe or detrimental habits in the bud. Use the guidance ahead to help you flourish as a maker.

Becoming friends with the axe

A carving axe is designed to tackle an array of duties from splitting large logs to carving intricate shavings. Before you start carving, you must split a log strategically multiple times to make a billet. From this, your project can be worked into a 'blank' – a crude, roughed-out initial 'sketch' of the outcome – with the axe. The blank is then sculpted and refined with knives into its final form.

The initial split occurs straight across the diameter of the end grain, and through the unstable pith. The pith and the juvenile wood are surrounded by tighter growth rings that dry out at a different rate compared to the larger rings towards the bark. To even out its drying process and to relieve tension, wood cracks towards the pith, opening the fibres and making it easier for the wood to match its environment. By splitting through it, you relieve a lot of tension in the wood and reduce the chances of the finished project cracking.

Parts of a carving axe
Carving axes come in many different shapes, weights and sizes but these key parts are usually common to all.

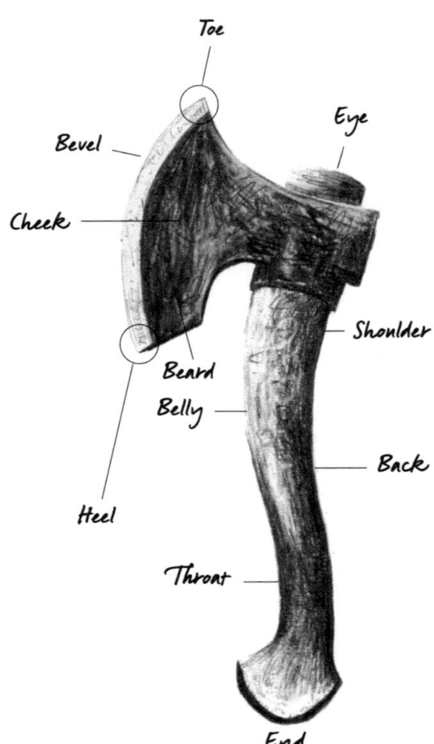

Splitting a log

Unlike processing firewood, where you can often simply use a big, hefty swing, your billet will need careful calculations. To get the best from a log, the axe should be deliberately placed and struck with a wooden club or heavy branch.

1. Ensure that your log is sat on a wooden block, and rest the axe edge across the diameter of the wood, through the pith. Hold the end of the handle in your non-dominant hand horizontally, as if you were holding the handlebar of a bicycle, as opposed to a fishing pole.

2. Step back slightly, keeping your feet away from the block, and strike down firmly on the back of the axe head with a wooden club to embed the edge into the end grain. Repeat until the log is open.

3. If the axe gets stuck, don't be tempted to hammer it out of the wood – it could suddenly dislodge: instead, try cleaving the wood by levering the axe as if to prise open the split. If it is still stuck, drive a wooden wedge into the split to safely free the axe with the opening of the log.

4. Larger rounds can be split using steel wedges while small branches can often be opened using a carving knife, and gently tapping on its spine with a mallet.

A log will likely have a small crack running through the pith at its weak spot, as if the tree is already letting you know how it wishes to be worked.

Starting to carve with the axe

An axe block can be worked at from a seated position, but you may feel in more control standing at an elevated block supported by three splayed legs. Split or branch-like legs can be wedged into pre-drilled holes at an angle of roughly 20 degrees to raise the stump from the floor.

A good stance

When standing at the axe block, your stance should be open with your non-dominant foot forward and dominant foot back, knees slightly bent. This encourages healthy posture and creates space between your dominant leg and the block, preventing an accident, should you miss the block.

Holding the axe

Find the balance point of the handle by placing your finger at the place where the axe head becomes the same weight as the rest of the axe handle. A full grip, clasped loosely around the handle, a centimetre or so back from the balance point, allows for the axe head to be slightly heavier. This means it requires less force in its downward cutting stroke.

Axe strokes

When carving, align the axe with your dominant shoulder, targeted to hit the centre of the axe block where the wood is presented to the axe at different angles by your other hand. Bringing your elbow close to your hip will remove the urge to revolve the axe, helping to maintain accuracy.

Raise the axe to a small height then drop your forearm holding the axe, with a pivot on your index finger to engage your wrist. Follow through completely into the axe block, not slowing your stroke, then lift again. When doing this stroke, the axe needs to oscillate on the pivot in order to engage the whole length of the axe bevel and slice through wood. It is not pushed from the shoulder or elbow like a saw, but manipulated in a way that moves the end of the axe handle as much as the head.

Axe cuts for carving

The three main axe cuts are shown here. As a general safety rule when carving with the axe, mentally divide the billet into two halves and always work within the boundary of the lower half so that your hand can safely grasp and manipulate the wood with fingers tucked back from the cutting face.

The relief cut

This cut gradually breaks up the fibres of a length of wood, impairing its structural integrity, making removal controlled and effortless towards a taper.

1. Start at the bottom of the billet, tilting the material away from the axe slightly, and create a series of incisions at about an inch in between each other up the length of the cutting face to the halfway point. These incisions are called relief cuts: broken fibres that fall away from the material.

2. Working from the halfway point, chase the material down to the axe block to remove it, forming a taper. To remove the material from the other half, simply turn the wood around and start within the other boundary. The relief cut is a gradual process and it may take a few passes to reach the desired outcome.

The end grain chop

Rounding the end of a billet is much tougher than working along its length because the tool needs to slice through the ends of the running fibres. A chop is required to effectively remove material where the wood is more resilient.

1. Hold the billet at its very end, fairly upright, tilting just slightly away from the axe. Cautiously raise the axe just a small amount beneath the level of your hand, then swing the axe firmly into the axe block, aiming to remove the very end corner of the billet exposed to the axe. It is helpful to do a few practice swings into the block to anticipate the blow before introducing the wood.

2. Once you have removed the initial chop, drop the hand holding the billet slowly, gradually arcing it further from the axe to increase the angle of the incision, and repeat the same axe chop. Like a second hand on a clock, continue to arc the billet away to round the end. The more chopping intervals you add to the arc, the more fluid the rounding will be.

The bump cut

The very end point of a billet can be prone to a tear out or split if axed too viciously with the end grain chop. A bump cut is a rather simple, controlled and fun technique that successfully tackles this problematic area.

1. Rest the axe edge onto the face of the billet on the piece of material you wish to remove. Hold both the axe and the end of the billet firmly and raise them up from the axe block together, maintaining their connection.

2. With a little force, sink them both firmly into the middle of the axe block to 'bump' the material away.

Grain direction

Wood grain is the assortment of wood fibres that form a tree. The grain structure can be imagined as a cluster of straws that stem along the length of a log. Despite the path of the straws meandering, interlocking and twisting occasionally around branches, burls and knots, they mainly follow the general direction of the trunk and branches.

Although trees and their growth patterns are wonderfully mysterious, the secrets to grain direction within a wooden three-dimensional shape are revealed in growth rings and the pin-striped patterns that run through wood. If you examine a sawn and milled wooden tabletop with a beautiful swirling grain that shows the movement of the wood, the pattern is caused by the wood bowing and twisting as it grew organically before it was sliced into a flat surface and uniform shape. Like a topographical map, you can begin to understand in which orientation the wood sat before it was cut. The grain on an object can be read like a hill or a staircase where the growth rings and patterns reveal height.

Direction of the carving knife

Understanding grain direction and the path that the knife needs to follow does not need to be complex. A carving knife carves in three ways: along the grain following the 'straws'; across the grain to round, flatten or burrow; and through the end of the grain where the fibres finish, to close and shorten.

The knife needs to work in a particular direction to freely pass through the wood and leave behind a smooth finish. This is called working with the grain. When working the knife in the opposite direction, against the grain, the knife is cutting into the ends of the straws and is being wedged and crammed into the fibres. It eventually gets stuck and embeds itself into the grain, leaving behind a jagged, untidy finish. It also can be unsafe to work against the grain because the knife requires a greater amount of force to drive through the wood, resulting in an uncontrolled follow-through.

A general rule for the knife is that it likes to travel down the steps of the grain and not up them. When the knife is descending with the grain, it will glide through the wood with ease, whereas if it climbs up the hill, it will catch and need to rest. It's a bit like a good hike where trekking down the mountain is much easier than scrambling up.

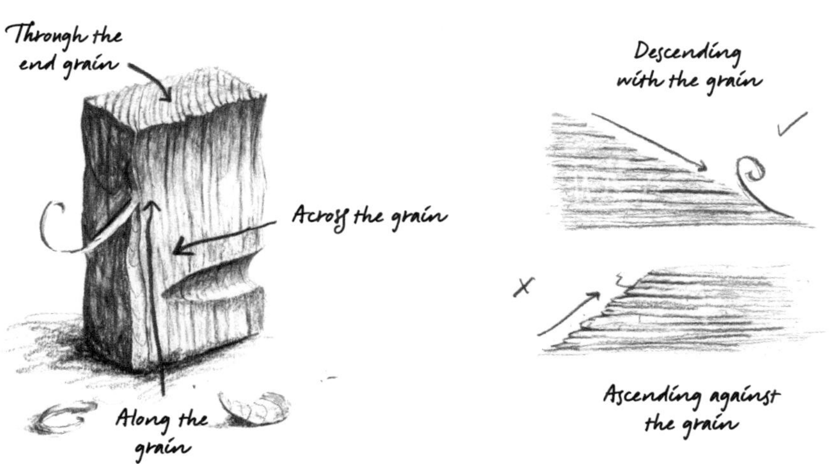

Getting to grips with the carving knife

Knowing when to apply different knife grips to specific areas of a project will come naturally with time and will slowly become more instinctive as the creative relationship between wood and carving deepens. A good grip also offers comfort and dexterity while guiding the knife safely away from your body and into the material. Each grip distributes the load of carving to specific muscles, offering a varying range of power.

It may initially be difficult to achieve a smooth finish. My advice is to use the grips to gain an understanding of where the bevel edge of the knife touches the wood: the difference between a messy and clean finish lies in the ability to keep the knife at a consistent angle through the duration of the cut.

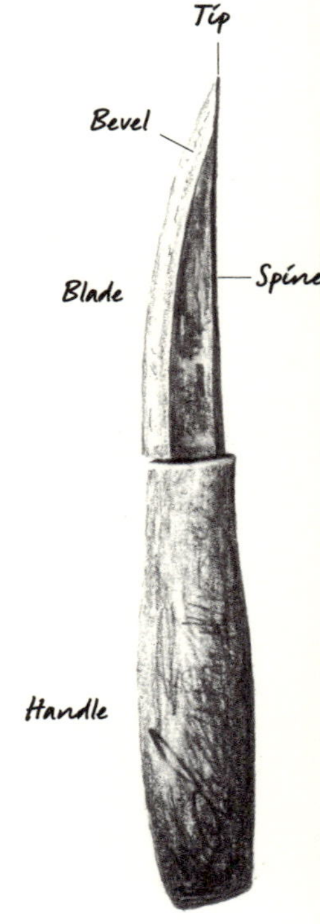

Parts of a carving knife

Learn the grips and make a tent peg

The five core grips on the following pages are known and practised widely by makers across the world, and are adapted for green woodworking. While carving a handy tent peg, you can practise all five grips. You'll need a 20cm (8in) long stick, 2–3cm (¾–1¼in) in diameter. Progress through the steps starting on page 51 and work through each grip until page 55.

Power grip

This grip is for making long shavings to remove the initial bulk at the beginning of a project. It uses the large muscle groups in your back and shoulders. Take your stick and focus on removing the bark and the first layer of sapwood.

1. In a seated position, place your knees and feet together, closing the legs. You will be carving the wood off to one side of your lap. Hold the knife in your dominant hand. In your non-dominant hand, hold the wood at one end and tilt it down towards the ground, across your lap. It is important that the wood is below the thigh for safety. Hold the knife in a full grip, forming a clenched fist. The blade should be facing towards the ground when held to your side, to meet the wood.

2. The power from this grip comes from the movement of the shoulder. To engage it fully, keep your dominant arm straight, with your elbow locked, squeezing the fist lightly so that the only moving part of the body is your shoulder.

3. Introduce the bevel edge to the side of the wood and find the knife's 'bite point' where it wants to begin cutting. Once you have found the bite, tilt the tip of the knife slightly up towards the sky to encourage a slice and, with a shrug, drop the shoulder to begin slowly driving the knife through the bark, revealing a shaving.

4. Once your shaving has been made, retract your shoulder up again towards your ear, twisting the piece of wood in your non-dominant hand to expose a new, untouched section. Repeat.

5. To remove material within the portion that you're holding, simply spin the stick around, hold the other end, and repeat the grip steps.

Pull grip

The pull grip slowly peels away long, controlled shavings. It is used to finesse the crude marks made by the power grip (see page 51) and is great for making long tapers or curves work more sculpturally with the grain. For this grip, refine the stick's surface into a smooth dowel.

1. In your non-dominant hand, bring the wood to a comfortable point at your sternum, pinching the end firmly with the fingertips for support. In your dominant hand, form a closed fist around the knife handle, blade pointing upwards with the cutting edge facing towards you, as if you're looking directly down the barrel of the knife.

2. Now transfer your thumb to the other side of the knife handle. It may seem strange to position it here, but it's safely tucked away and does a great job of providing extra support within the twist of the grip, increasing knife control.

3. Next, position the knife upright to the outward-facing side, beneath your fingertips. Your non-dominant hand should always be the farthest point away and the knife shouldn't ever be positioned ahead of your fingers. Angle the knife so that the tip is directed away – this enhances the slicing motion when it comes to making a shaving, and increases the safety.

4. Draw the knife back gradually, revealing a gentle spiral like a ribbon shaving. The knife's pace is regulated, being naturally slowed by your body, with the tip always upright and angled away, all while the wood shields your non-dominant hand.

5. Focus on applying a steady, consistent movement, drawing back from the elbow, brushing your forearm against your hip. Look down the knife's edge. Focus on the angle with which the bevel is being introduced to the wood. How consistently can you keep the knife at this angle? How long can you make a paper-thin shaving? How smooth can you make the surface?

Chest lever grip

This grip is good for driving through areas of the wood with a higher resistance, such as the ends of your project where the grain runs out, or the heartwood. It is one of the trickier grips to learn and applies some pressure to your chest. Explore different upper-body hand placements for more comfort. Use this grip to bring the end of your dowel into a sharp point.

1. Sit comfortably with your back straight, hands open on your lap, palms facing upwards. Hold the knife in your dominant hand, with the blade ahead of the index finger, its cutting edge pointing away from the centre of your body. Hold the stick in your other palm, with the end you want to carve ahead of your hand. From here, close your hands, gripping the two objects from underneath. You should be able to see all of your fingernails.

2. Cross the knife on top of the wood to form an 'X' shape. Bring the whole grip into your chest so that the knuckles of your little fingers are touching your ribs. Stick your arms out like wings, making a straight line from elbow to elbow. Use your chest as a lever for your hands, stemming from the articulation of your shoulders.

3. Bring your elbows forward slightly and dig the knife blade into the top of the wood until you feel resistance of the fibres. Stiffen your wrists by squeezing the knife and the wood at the same time. Bring your elbows back and puff your chest out to powerfully lever a shaving away.

4. Take your time to really engage your elbows and shoulders (not the wrist) to pivot against your chest. This maximizes the power by using a wider radius and stronger muscle group than your wrist can offer. As you gain confidence, your hands may change position and deviate from the cradle you had at the start. Try to maintain it because it helps keep your wrist rigid. Rotate the piece in your hand to expose a new area to the knife.

Thumb push grip

The thumb push grip removes targeted chips of wood, making it perfect for finishing touches, refinement and decorative details. Use this grip to refine the spike of the peg into a fine point and add a notch to catch a guide rope.

1. Hold the stick in your non-dominant hand in a position where you can reach the spiked end to push the knife away with your thumb.

2. Now, as if you are sharpening a pencil, use your thumb to guide the back of the knife onto the wood. For safety and comfort, push the knife at the end of the handle where it meets the metal as opposed to the spine of the blade. Not only will this part of the knife, with its wider surface, prevent blisters, it will also protect your hand from the cutting edge if the knife is accidentally facing the wrong way.

3. Repeat while rotating the wood to different areas. That's pretty much the gist of this grip. It's really simple and puts you in a confident place to make direct decisions of where to remove material. This grip can be applied more or less anywhere on a whittling project. If you can push the piece of wood you want to remove with your thumb, you can remove it with the knife.

4. You can also use this grip to establish a notch for a guide rope to cling to. About 2.5cm (1in) from the blunt end of the stick, push the knife directly into the wood's top surface to make an incision. Next, spin the piece of wood around and whittle back a shaving into the incision to create a notch. Repeat over again to add depth to the valley. This style of cut where a shaving meets an incision is called a stop cut.

Note
For safety, the thumb push grip should always be directed pushing away from you, and not towards; always rotate the project to practise correctly.

Apple peeler grip

This grip is performed much like you would peel an apple. It focuses on squeezing the dominant hand into a fist to cut with the knife, using the thumb as an anchor. It is great for establishing a chamfer, a softer 45-degree facet in between the sharp 90-degree edge where two sides meet. On wood, this gives a little more longevity to the edge and contributes to a comfortable, considered finish that is perfect for the blunt end of your peg. This grip can also be used in collaboration with the thumb push grip (see opposite) to add decorative details.

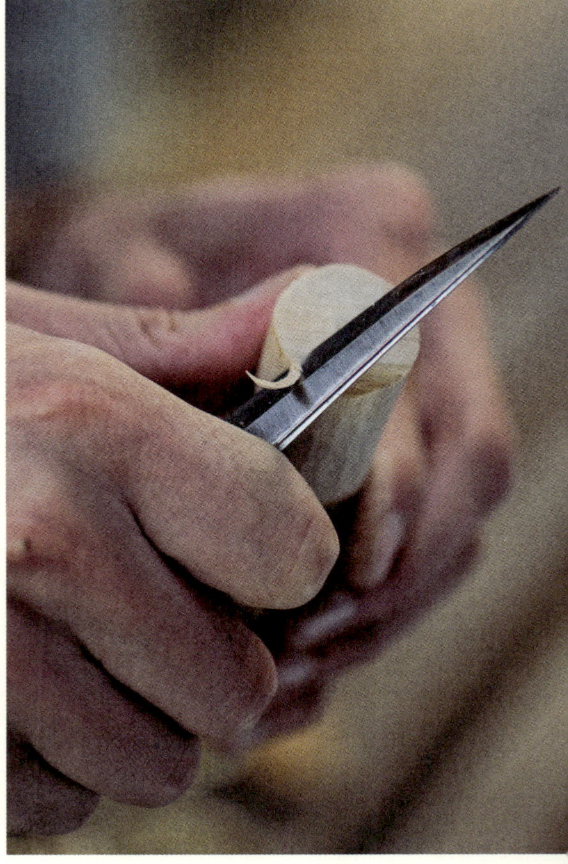

1. Firmly hold the stick upright in your non-dominant hand, exposing the blunt end.

2. The focus here is on your dominant, knife hand. Practise for a moment how it feels to hold the knife in the clutch of your fingers with your hand slightly open, and then closing it into a fist, moving the knife back and forth as if to peel the skin from an apple.

3. This motion should free up your thumb, which can serve as an anchor, safely latching on to the side of the stick, providing purchase for the knife to carve through the wood.

4. Apply this to the blunt end of the stick. Try squeezing away a consistent 45-degree facet around the edge of the dowel.

I like to have a carving stick or block to hand like a sketchbook, referring back to the grips occasionally like a mindfulness or yoga practice to grow my skills and centre my mind.

Using the hook knife

The articulation of a hook knife (also known as a spoon knife) can be hard to grasp because it requires a lot of coordination. Practising on a spare offcut of wood can really help to gain a better understanding of how the hook knife functions before making a spoon or bowl.

Basic hollowing across the grain

Start with the apple peeler grip (see page 55), with the hook knife in the clutch of your dominant hand, the hook facing upwards so it is able to rotate and coil with the closure of the fist. Use the thumb as an anchor to latch on to the side of the project and support your grip, unexposed beneath the lip. Close and squeeze your fist gently as your wrist rotates away, to encourage a sweeping motion to excavate material.

Hook knife bevel angles vary, depending on a knife's manufacture and style. Begin by skimming the surface in the middle of the targeted area, to gain an understanding of where the bevel meets the wood, working across the grain within a small circumference to establish the beginnings of a hollow. Now expand and amplify the hollow by entering the tool earlier, exaggerating the articulation, and exiting the tool later.

Once the desired width is set, the hook knife can then burrow deeper by working from edge to edge in a constant sweep, forming longer shavings. The consistency of the angle in relation to the shape of the concave is key to a smooth finish. If the knife is leaving behind chattering marks, it is being introduced to the wood at a steeper, unfamiliar angle in relation to the hollow.

Advanced hollowing with the grain

Hollowing with the grain leaves a smoother finish. Though harder to grasp, the finish can elevate eating spoons, making them much more comfortable against the mouth when in use.

To work with the grain, use your non-dominant hand to cradle and grasp the project from underneath. Above the lip, expose three fingers from the surface near the hollow. In your dominant hand, the knife can pivot against the exposed fingers in an arc, stemming from the rise of the elbow to carve down into the bottom of the concave bowl.

The hook knife can only carve down from the lip into the bowl and not back up the other side as the overlapping grain on the opposite wall prevents the knife from escaping. The project will need to be rotated in the palm to carve back down to meet the previous shaving.

Getting the fibres to meet in the middle of the hollow can be very difficult. More often than not, there will likely be a bit of a mess in the bottom of the bowl. A final sweep across the grain will tidy up any stray fibres. Carving with the grain requires much more dexterity and knife confidence but will ultimately give a much cleaner and more refined hollow. For safety, it is important to only expose the fingers that are used to pivot against the knife and keep the rest behind the spine of the knife, out of the way.

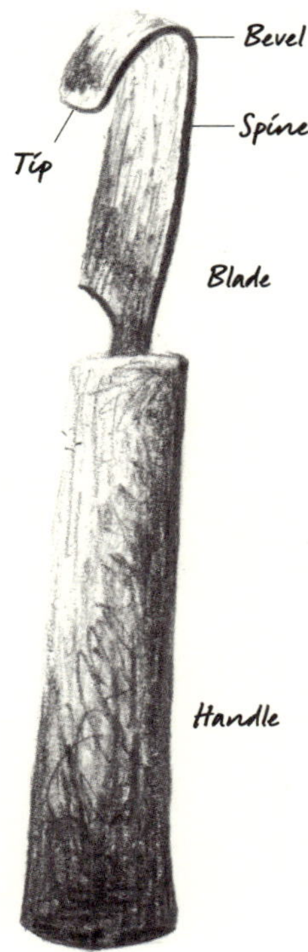

Parts of a hook knife

Carving projects

I have designed each one of these projects to be fun and explorative. I hope you find them to be meditative, open ended and full of possibilities. Try not to strive for perfection; it may take a few attempts to make pieces that you are happy with. Start with the first project, building your skills with each outcome, graduating to the next one and slowly surrounding yourself with heirlooms and artefacts of time well spent.

Mini bud vase

I like to collect things on my walks: stones, shells, acorns, even the seeds from the apples I eat along the way. Most of all, I like to pick flowers. A bud vase is a small container to hold your tiny bouquets, presenting them for yourself and others to encounter around the home. This project is a celebration of nature, a nod to what it means to stop and notice our relationship with things that grow.

I usually make bud vases from offcuts from the larger pieces I create, or from interesting pieces of wood that, although maybe too gnarly for some projects, still took the time and courage to grow. Making the vase is relatively straightforward and offers a vast sense of sculptural freedom. The only necessity is to ensure that it has a drilled hole in the top to hold a flower.

Toolkit and materials

- An axe or splitting tool and wooden club, bench hook, saw, ruler, pencil, elastic band, drill with a 6mm (¼in) drill bit, adjustable pliers, clamp or vice and a sharp carving knife.
- Small branch, segment or offcut of fresh wood, anything from 6cm (2½in) cubed or greater.

How to make a bud vase

1. If needed, split your piece of wood to around 5cm (2in) in diameter or greater. While resting on a bench hook, saw to a 6cm (2½in) length. With waste wood, you may need to saw an end back a little if the wood has begun to dry and displays signs of cracking.

2. Draw a loose pebble shape on the end grain. With an axe and club, gently split away any excess material that falls outside of the shape to reveal a rough, cylindrical blank.

3. Next, decide which way up your vase is going to sit. Perhaps there is a particularly nice feature or colouring to the wood that you wish to highlight towards the top. Once decided, mark with the pencil on the top end grain where you wish to drill the mouth of the vase, where the flowers are held. For a more organic feel, place it off-centre.

4. On a drill bit, measure and mark 3cm (1¼in) from the cutting end with a tied elastic band. While either holding the block of wood with a pair of adjustable pliers (if you have an electric drill) or clamping the wood to a workbench, drill a hole straight into the end grain up to the elastic band depth indicator.

Be mindful of your capabilities while carving. Knowing when to stop and put the tools down can be difficult to gauge. Listen to your body.

5. With a carving knife, use the apple peeler grip (see page 55) to refine the overall cylinder so that the split and cleft surface is smooth and rounded.

6. Draw another smaller pebble shape in the middle of the base end of the blank, roughly 2cm (¾in) in diameter. Next, draw a collar around the circumference of the cylinder, about 1cm (⅜in) from the base. From this line, using the apple peeler grip again, you can begin to round and roll the edge into the base carefully towards the 2cm (¾in) pebble, forming the bottom of a bulb shape.

7. With a combination of the thumb push (see page 54) and the apple peeler grip, begin to taper up with your knife towards the mouth. To achieve the asymmetric pear-looking shape, taper one side of the pear's profile a little steeper for a more organic aesthetic.

8. For finishing touches, add more facets to refine the shape, making it appear smoother and more intricate looking. A thin rim will add a sense of elegance to the overall shape.

Thoughts on

The harmony of making

Over time, your carving will start to become more intuitive and skills will begin to grow and flourish as levels of dexterity increase. There will be times where your mind will begin to harmonize with your making. Fear of injury will slowly fade and your outcomes will be noticeably smoother and more refined.

Distractions will slowly dwindle, time and space will become less important as your brain relaxes into a meditative state. The past simply becomes the past, the future seems far away and will occur when it needs to and the present begins to fill the mind: a familiar pool that is to be stepped into and bathed in as wood chips fall to the ground. This 'flow state' when immersed in making is relatable to yoga, breathwork, guided meditation and massage.

The rhythmic passing of the knife through the fibres of wood is like a relaxing pulse that can be focused on. Like breathwork, knife grips can be practised and trained with patience and discipline to create satisfying, curly shavings.

For many makers, craft is an outlet – a tactile response to complex hurdles, a way of creatively processing thoughts and minimizing stress, all while gaining a sense of achievement. Carving is a reduction process of deliberate decision making to unravel an outcome from a natural material full of unique quirks. It can teach themes of letting go for the many who find it difficult to move forward.

Above all, green woodcarving belongs to all as a craft that celebrates individuality, self-improvement and tradition. There is great therapy in being able to use simple hand tools to manipulate wood into a form. When carving, we can be far away from the noise of everyday life.

Butter spreader

A wooden butter spreader is a pleasingly tactile piece of Scandinavian tableware. It incorporates a flowing taper transition from blade to handle, with the grain of the wood running through for strength. A tapering head and fine edge make ease out of brushing a lump of butter onto a piece of toast. Carving a butter spreader is a fun project to explore the combination of both functionality and pleasing design.

As many butter spreader billets can be harvested from one piece of wood, you can play with a variety of shapes and forms. I like to think beyond the butter and into the realms of other spreadable delights. Could you make the perfect jam smearer? How can you get into the corners of the jar? This is a fantastic opportunity to loosen up into fun shapes and let the imagination flow.

Toolkit and materials

• An axe and wooden club, pencil and a sharp carving knife.

• Fresh round of hardwood, a minimum of 10cm (4in) in diameter and roughly 20cm (8in) in length.

How to make a butter spreader

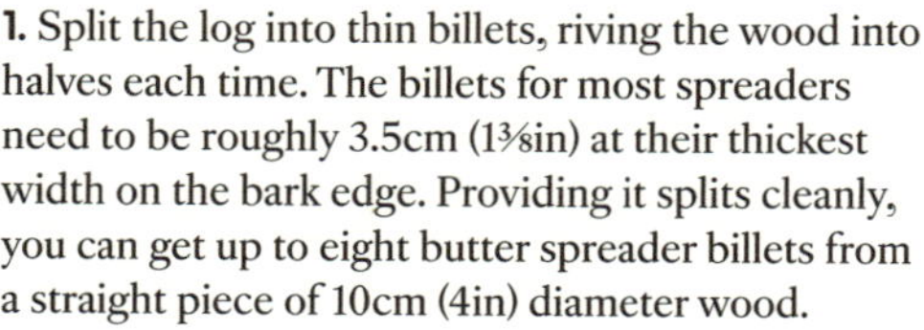

1. Split the log into thin billets, riving the wood into halves each time. The billets for most spreaders need to be roughly 3.5cm (1⅜in) at their thickest width on the bark edge. Providing it splits cleanly, you can get up to eight butter spreader billets from a straight piece of 10cm (4in) diameter wood.

2. Choose your favourite billet (the rest can be used for more spreaders later). With the axe, use the relief cut (see page 46) to carve away the sharp pith edge, removing approximately 1cm (⅜in) of material. Because the pith is unstable and prone to splitting, it is good practice to remove it early on.

3. Use the carving knife to flatten the surfaces on both of the cleft faces of the billet. The chest lever grip (see page 53) will make quick work of the raised fibres, reducing the material to create a smooth plane.

4. Draw on your chosen design with pencil, incorporating the grain. (See page 74 for some design tips.)

When designing a piece, I like to encourage working freehand, taking inspiration from the environment, nature and mood.

Designing for strength and beauty

The spreader will need to follow some basic rules to ensure that it functions well. It must be able to stand up to the stress of everyday use so, for strength, the grain should run through the shape from the handle to the tip. The main stress of the utensil is on the section where the blade meets the handle. Leaving a portion of material behind in this area will give the spreader longevity. Most butter spreader designs have a handle length of about 10cm (4in) before they flow into the blade. If this is your first spreader, keep the shape simple and keep the spine relatively straight to ease yourself in.

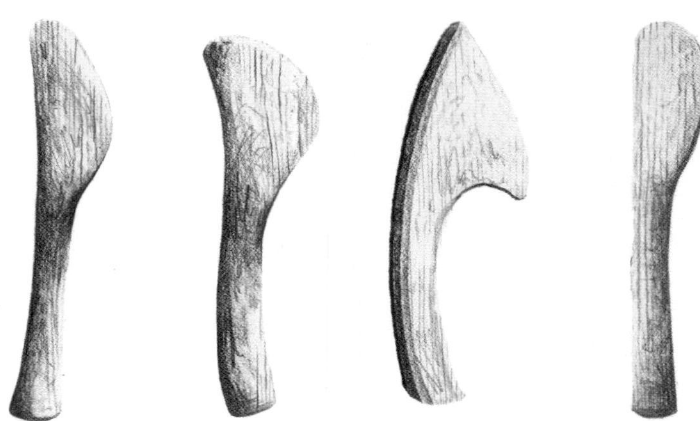

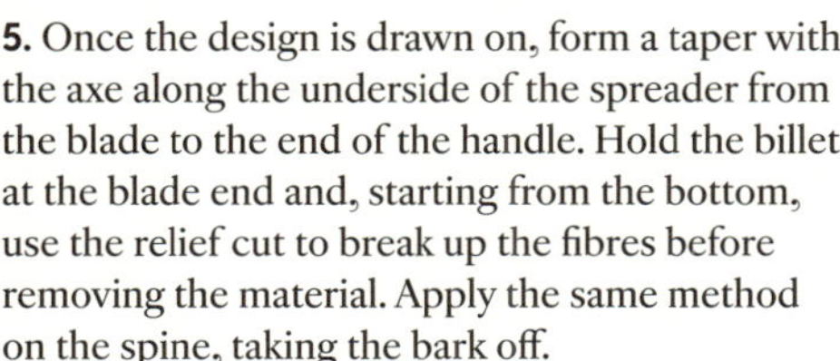

5. Once the design is drawn on, form a taper with the axe along the underside of the spreader from the blade to the end of the handle. Hold the billet at the blade end and, starting from the bottom, use the relief cut to break up the fibres before removing the material. Apply the same method on the spine, taking the bark off.

6. Draw a centreline along the back of the spine and mark with a cross the point where the handle becomes the blade. With the axe, thin the billet on either side of the blade, leaving about 0.5cm (3/16in) either side of the centreline. Redraw the shape of the blade where you have cut it away.

7. Now use the end grain chop technique (see page 47) to round the tip of the spreader blade, gradually arching the blank away from the axe to increase the angle.

8. With a carving knife, use the power grip (see page 51) to refine the spreader's blade, thinning it towards the spreading edge to a width no smaller than 2mm (⅛in).

9. Study the grain and how it runs through the pencil drawing. Using the chest lever grip, flow the underside of the knife into the handle. Now carve and refine the spreader's spine using the drawing grip, slowly peeling back long shavings to a desired handle thickness.

10. With a combination of the thumb push (see page 54) and the pull grip (see page 52) begin to enhance the spreader with smooth facets. Be sure to keep testing it to see how it feels in the hand when in use. To round the tip of the spreader use the apple peeler grip (see page 55).

11. Lastly, combine the thumb push and the apple peeler grips to chamfer the edges on the handle's end and along the length of the spreader's blade.

Thoughts on

Documenting

Woodcarving is an intimate practice, full of individuality and sensitivity. Though it may be daunting to share such a personal journey, documenting pieces can be a useful way of analysing your craft and celebrating a carving's existence before parting with it. I enjoy creating a home studio set-up to artistically shoot the pieces I've made as I imagined while carving them. Photographs soon accumulate into archives of past works while drawings and writings become sketchbooks bursting with inspiration and ideas.

My enthusiasm for documenting my work stems from having no evidence of my first carved pieces. They were spoons, crudely made from pieces of seasoned firewood, given away as soon as they were made, without knowing how important they might be to me. I would love to meet them again, to observe the small sparks of creativity that lit the blazing fire, which still fuels my carvings today.

I recognize carving as an artform that is well paired with a sketchbook. Writing about my process and sketching new ideas is a useful way to contain my enthusiasm and awaken new ideas. When unloading my thoughts, I find myself often documenting my surroundings and environment with pressed flowers, drawings, instinctive thoughts or poetry. Though sometimes it isn't obvious, they often somehow make their way into the shapes I make.

End grain buttons

When did you last pause to appreciate the humble button? They have a lot more heritage than you might think, with some estimated to be over 5,000 years old. I enjoy carving buttons to replace plastic ones and I love the way a carved item can add a sprinkle of joy to something as humdrum as getting dressed.

Button making is a wonderfully quick and clever way of exploring small-scale repetition with many outcomes. Shapes are determined by the overall profile of a length of wood that is sliced to make many buttons of the same diameter, pattern and tone of wood.

Toolkit and materials

• A template, made from cardboard, a fraction larger than the size of the button you intend to make.

• An axe and club, pencil, sharp carving knife, vice or clamp, drill with a small drill bit, pull-cut saw and bench hook (optional).

• 30cm (12in) long round of wood, wide enough to fit the size of the template between the pith and the bark.

How to make a button

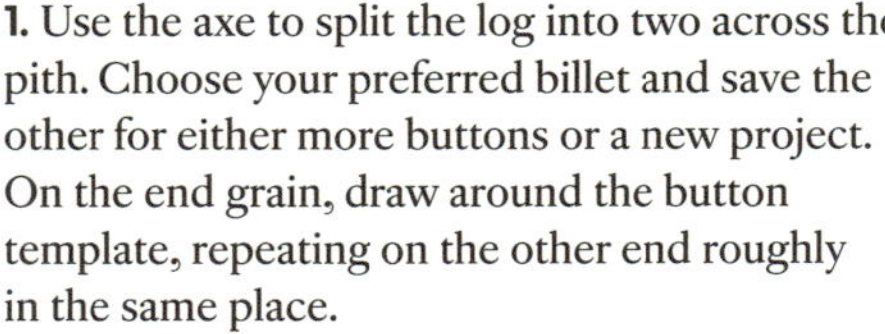

1. Use the axe to split the log into two across the pith. Choose your preferred billet and save the other for either more buttons or a new project. On the end grain, draw around the button template, repeating on the other end roughly in the same place.

2. Still using the axe, sculpt the billet into a cylinder. Begin on the bark side, using relief cuts (see page 46) to break up the fibres from the bottom of the billet to its halfway point, reducing down to the first layer of wood to meet the pencil drawing. Repeat on the opposite face. To ensure a straight result, lay the billet on a flat surface to see if it sits flush. Repeat this process for the two remaining pronounced corners, biting the axe into the sharp edges to form the relief cut. Repeat again on the next most pronounced corner, gradually turning the prism into a multi-faceted cylinder.

3. Clamp the wood upright in a vice, or brace it with a clamp against a table leg. On the end grain, mark the hole positions with a pencil. Place them a reasonable distance apart to prevent them from tearing into each other when drilled. Traditionally, buttons have four holes in a square format. The holes are drilled at this point in case the outer surface is marked when clamped and because the large facets created by the axe make for a better texture and shape for clamping securely.

4. Drill the holes to an even depth. Drilling straight can be difficult but I find that positioning the wood upright makes it easier. If you are drilling holes bigger than 4mm (5⁄32in), I recommend first drilling thinner pilot holes as the end grain can be tough.

5. With the carving knife, refine the cylinder's surface with the power grip (see page 51), turning the axe marks into smooth knife facets. If desired, you can also develop a much smoother finish using the pull grip (see page 52).

6. Shave the top face of the cylinder using the apple peeler grip (see page 55). Use the same grip or the thumb push grip (see page 54) to slightly chamfer and round off the end of the cylinder. This will be the front face of the first button.

I find the button-making process not only to be very mindful and gentle, but also a thoughtful way to add new life to a worn garment.

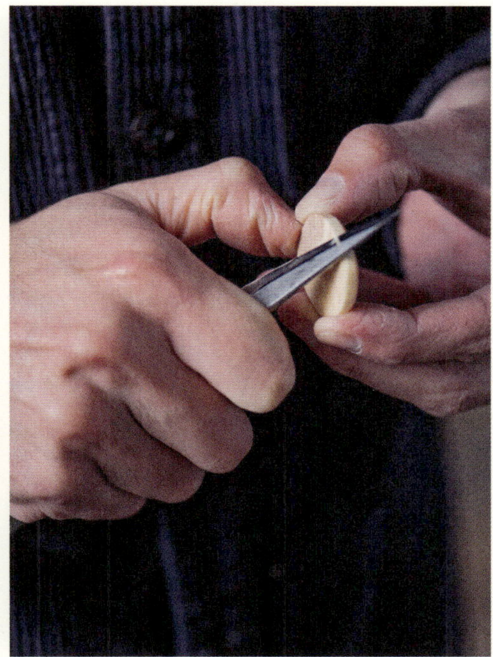

7. While holding the cylinder firmly at the end of a worktop or in a bench hook, saw off the button, using a pull-cut saw, to your desired thickness.

8. Once freed, the back of the button may be a little jagged and will require a chamfered edge where it meets the side. Repeat the previous step until you need to drill more holes, run out of wood or have enough buttons!

Branch hook

Where else would a woodcarver hang their hat after a long day of making other than on their very own branch hook? Fallen or pruned branches with shooting intersections can be made into useful hooks, installed in select places around the home, with a charming nod to wildness. These branches can be found almost anywhere where there are trees. After a windy storm, forest floors are sometimes full of suitable branch wood, making this a great excuse to get outside and embark on a foraging trip to find some.

Toolkit and materials

• A pull-cut saw, axe and club, sharp carving knife, pencil, clamp or vice and a drill with a 4mm (5⁄32in) drill bit.

• A branch or limb with an intersection or two. The main limb needs to be relatively straight in relation to its upwards shooting twig offspring. The foraged branch needs to be green and fresh, not brittle or rotten.

How to make a branch hook

1. Prune your branch and intersection to an appropriate length. An effective hook will protrude at least 5cm (2in) from the parent branch. Depending on the thickness, I would estimate that most hooks need to be about 8cm (3in) long to successfully hold a wide range of items. The branch that supports the hook needs to also be a suitable length to be screwed easily into a wall and support the gravitational load of an object pulling for long periods of time. Beneath the hook, the parent branch needs to be at least 4cm (1½in) long to house a screw. Above, I recommend a length greater than 4cm (1½in) from the distance where the tip of the hook reaches in relation to the parent branch to counteract a pivotal force.

2. Split the parent branch in half with the axe, across the pith, directly behind the protruding hook with the aim that it will sit flush against a surface when the hook sticks outwards. It is likely that your branch is bowed. This is no cause for concern and will be rectified later.

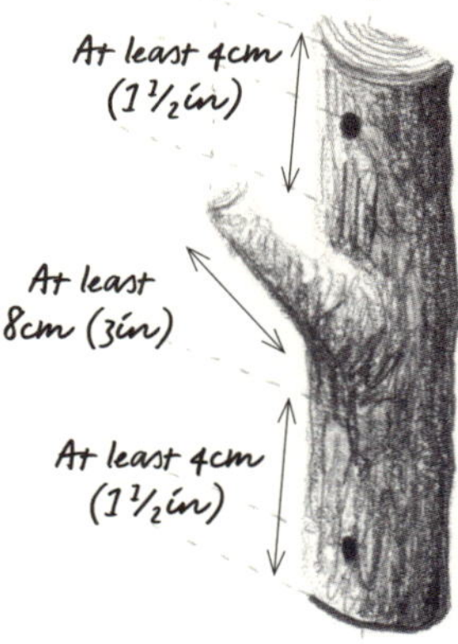

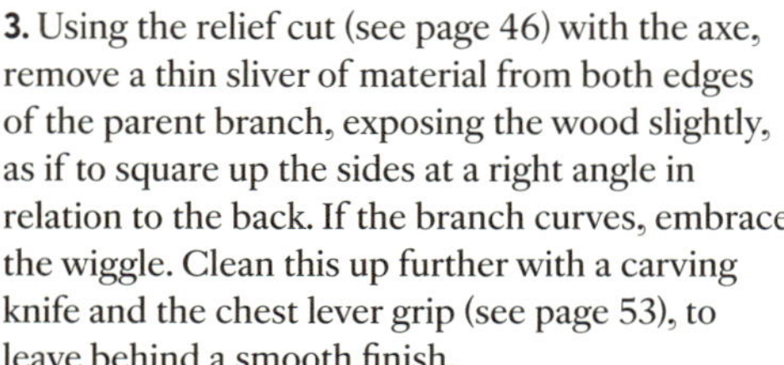

3. Using the relief cut (see page 46) with the axe, remove a thin sliver of material from both edges of the parent branch, exposing the wood slightly, as if to square up the sides at a right angle in relation to the back. If the branch curves, embrace the wiggle. Clean this up further with a carving knife and the chest lever grip (see page 53), to leave behind a smooth finish.

4. Place the hook on a flat surface and, while resting your pencil flat, draw a line around the perimeter of the parent branch to establish a straight rule. Depending on the severity of the bow, you may need to add a block under the pencil to account for the gap between surface and branch.

I like to imagine a slow, considered walking pace in between each axe blow to allow a thought and a breath before safely removing more material.

5. With the axe, use the relief cut to remove the material that is marked on the parent branch in order to make it flat.

6. Now that the back is flat, carve away the bark to reveal the wood underneath. Since you are not altering the natural shape of the branch, most of the material will be fairly straightforward to whittle away. I suggest using a combination of the chest lever and the thumb push grip (see page 54) to tackle most of the hook. The trickiest section is the ridge: the tight gap where the angle of the protruding stick meets the nook. This can be worked with the pull grip (see page 52), adding a twist of the wrist, following the cramped curve of the ridge while carefully engaging the agile tip of the knife.

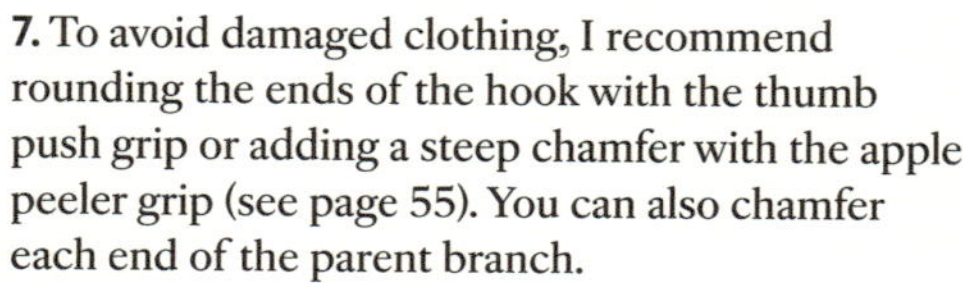

7. To avoid damaged clothing, I recommend rounding the ends of the hook with the thumb push grip or adding a steep chamfer with the apple peeler grip (see page 55). You can also chamfer each end of the parent branch.

8. Drill a hole at the top and bottom of the parent branch. While most screws will fit comfortably in a 4mm (5/32in) drilled hole, you may need other sizes if you are using specific screws. The screw needs to slide comfortably within the pocket with the head being too big to pass through in order to brace it against a wall. If you are using a hand-powered drill, carefully clamp the hook in a vice or against a worktop, with a piece of sacrificial wood between so that you don't ruin the carving or the worktop. I recommend both holes to be at least 2cm (3/4in) from both ends. Sit the top screw higher than the protruding branch so it can be accessed when screwing into the wall. In case of a tear out, drill into the wood from the front to avoid any damage to the carved surface. Wait for the hook to dry (see page 145) before attaching it to the wall.

Thoughts on

Giving and selling

Each of your carved creations is a capsule of energy and time. Gifting these to others can bring mountains of joy and serotonin, and it won't be long before you encounter your pieces again – be it a bowl cradling precious ornaments, or a spoon sitting centre stage in a utensil pot. There is a generous swapping culture among many green woodworkers. Trading feels like an exchange of letters, written in a secret dialect that only a woodcarver can interpret, and it may not be long before these carved correspondences can be seen dotted around your home.

Selling your work also grants others the opportunity to share in your artistic voice. It took me a long time to become comfortable selling my wares, but I have come to understand that craft skills are to be deeply valued. The wooden spoon that goes home with someone is a genuinely good product that cannot be fully replicated again, and should be priced and sold respectfully. Consider the value of carving time for yourself and other makers. Not only are we full-time makers carving beautiful shapes and forms, but we are also dedicated to truly expressing ourselves for a living.

There are many places to sell your carvings, but nothing beats selling in person at a market stall. Being able to meet the people who take home your goods, inviting them into your process and sharing your knowledge, is deeply rewarding and may inspire more makers to embark on their own craft journey.

Fibre brush

On your carving journey, you will likely find wood chips in the most curious of places: pockets, teacups, even in beds. Making a wooden brush from foraged wood and natural bristles can transform a mundane cleaning experience into something grounding and peaceful.

This style of brush is very successful at sweeping up shavings and makes good use of wood, with little waste. The technique to attach the bristles is universal and I invite you to take the learnings from this exercise to explore unique shapes to further your own personal style.

Toolkit and materials

• An axe and club, pencil, sharp carving knife, clamp or vice, cloth, masking tape, drill with 6mm (¼in) drill bit, cotton thread, epoxy resin or wood glue and scissors.

• Natural fibres (see page 104) and a nice, branchy piece of wood, about 20cm (8in) in length and roughly 5cm (2in) in diameter (can make two handles).

• A simple gauge to measure the correct amount of fibres to insert into pre-drilled holes in the handle – a dry piece of waste wood with a 6mm (¼in) hole through it should work just fine.

How to make a brush

1. Split the wood into two halves across the pith with the axe and club. Using the relief cut (see page 46) with the axe, shave a small section of the cleft surface to reduce the face of one of the halves, removing any pith material.

2. With a pencil, draw a centreline that follows the grain through the middle of the axed surface. Draw two more lines that run roughly 1.5cm (½in) either side of the centreline.

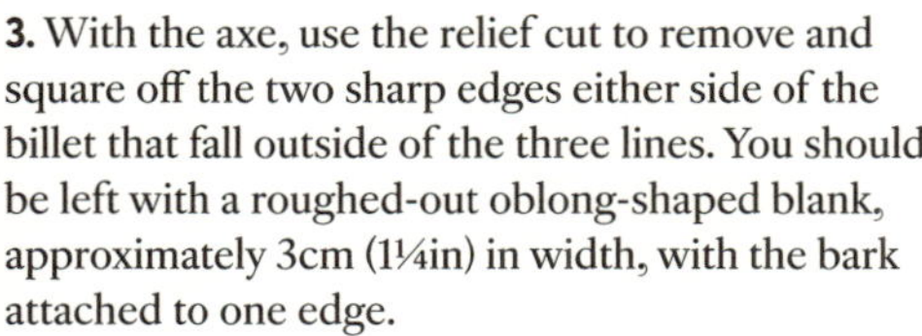

3. With the axe, use the relief cut to remove and square off the two sharp edges either side of the billet that fall outside of the three lines. You should be left with a roughed-out oblong-shaped blank, approximately 3cm (1¼in) in width, with the bark attached to one edge.

4. Now refine the billet into a more rounded form. With a carving knife, engage the power grip (see page 51) on the four sharp corners along the length of the oblong shape, turning it into an octagonal prism. When using the power grip, remember to work halfway down in one direction, then flip the billet around to work halfway down the other.

5. Continue to use the power grip to begin carving the octagonal prism into a more rounded shape. If needed, refine the curve further, employing a steady pull grip (see page 52) to slowly draw back a long shaving. For the ends where the pull grip couldn't quite reach, finish with the chest lever or the thumb push grip (see pages 53 and 54). On the back of the handle, I like to leave the bark surface intact, or if the bark falls off, I retain the live edge texture of the wood beneath along the spine of the handle.

6. Now that the handle has been rounded to your preference, use the thumb push grip to chamfer the edges on the end grain. Once complete, place the handle into a paper bag with some wood chips to dry slowly for a week or so. Drying the piece before fitting the bristles will allow for any shrinkage or warping and for a better adhesion to the bristles when they are installed.

Leaving a strip of bark on the handle allows the smooth finish of the carved wood to juxtapose with the gnarly texture of the tree it came from, bringing us a little closer to nature while using this everyday object.

7. Once the handle is dry, draw a new centreline along the underside, opposite the strip of bark. Towards one end, draw seven indicators along the line, 1cm (⅜in) apart, to mark where to drill.

8. Even if you have an electric hand drill, clamping the wood will give you much more accuracy. Pre-wrap the sides of the piece in a cloth before clamping to prevent any defects. Clamp the piece firmly in a vice or onto a flat surface. To drill the holes at the same depth, create a marker with some masking tape around the drill bit to a depth of 1cm (⅜in). Drill the holes down to the tape.

9. Using the pull grip, plane off a thin shaving to remove the pencil marks and any raised fibres made from the previous step. Use the thumb push grip to reach the very ends of the brush handle.

10. Fill the 6mm (¼in) bristle gauge with fibres until it can hold no more. Bring the fibres into the middle of the gauge and tap the end of the bundle to flatten. Wrap the bundle a few times with the cotton thread and tie a tight knot. Trim the loose ends close to the thread and repeat six times.

Natural fibres

Natural fibres are not something commonly sold in stores and may need to be foraged or sourced online. I like to prepare mine from nettles. They are wonderfully versatile for both bristles and twine and can be harvested in the summer months. While wearing gardening gloves, nettles can be cut cleanly from the ground and stripped by running a clenched fist from top to bottom to remove the leaves and spikes. Once removed, the gloves can come off and the nettles can be split by hand and peeled away from their pith. Once separated, they can then be split into small fibres and dried.

Both pine and coconut fibres are quite strong and coarse but often warp and lose their shape over time. Tampico bristles, traditionally harvested from the Mexican agave plant, are strong, soft and durable all-round fibres, sustainably sold in small quantities. Note that when glueing in the natural fibre, the wood will need to be dry to adhere correctly. Though this wait time can be tedious, I do find it something to look forward to. A wait time tends to encourage me to work in small batches, dedicating more time to each stage of the process, repeating favourite shapes to make a small collection of brushes.

11. Pour a few drops of epoxy or wood glue into one of the holes and stuff it with the flat end of the tied fibres. Repeat for each hole, one at a time so the glue doesn't cure before reaching the end. With the scissors, release the cotton ties and allow some time for the glue to dry.

12. In a neat line, cut the ends of the bristles to a desired length, combing out any loose strands. Sweep up the mess!

Thoughts on

Leaving things behind

Woodcarving is a process of slow reduction. Each outcome is an accumulation of choices to remove pieces of wood in response to the material and the design. Not only is there a great level of skill needed to be able to effectively remove material with a carving knife, but there is artistry in the ability to make decisions to sensitively leave things behind.

A tree grows uniquely and gently with beautiful characteristics and imperfections. Building a connection with wood and reading it in a way that incorporates its quirks takes time. I am constantly in awe of how trees grow, how they reveal stories and traits that display personality. Sometimes I feel as if the tree is wanting to collaborate with me. Often it is apparent that the wood wants to leave something behind: a live edge, a piece of bark, a knot, its asymmetry or colour.

Carving is also deeply unforgiving – you cannot put back a piece of wood that has been removed. Leaving behind big, decisive tool marks often expresses bravery, anger and confidence whereas small, meticulous tool marks echo themes of patience, stillness and refinement. Noticing the energy spent on a piece can sometimes feel like staring into a maker's self portrait.

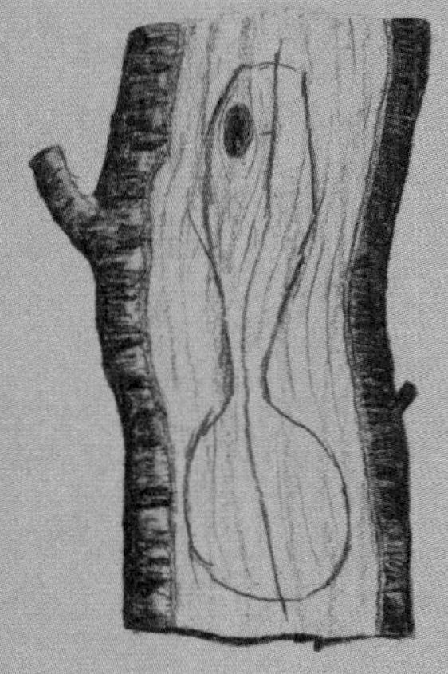

Small bark-up bowl

Throughout history, the bowl has been portrayed in many forms, shapes and sizes for different uses – from long, flat kneading dough bowls to intricately ornate bowls for ceremonially sharing ale. Wooden bowls are traditionally made from half of a split log and can be carved from either the pith side or the bark side up. Working into the wood from the bark surface creates a sweeping rim as the wood curves, which is wonderfully decorative, stronger and favoured by many woodcarvers. Unlike spoons, the carved bowl's shape is mainly determined firstly by the hollow itself. These traditional Swedish-style 'bark-up' bowls have a handle on either side of the end grain, like ears, to grasp hold of when in use.

Toolkit and materials

• An axe and club, sharp carving knife, pencil, compass (optional), hook knife and a pull-cut saw.

• Log, free from knots, no larger than 9cm (3½in) in diameter, roughly 25cm (10in) or so in length.

How to make a bark-up bowl

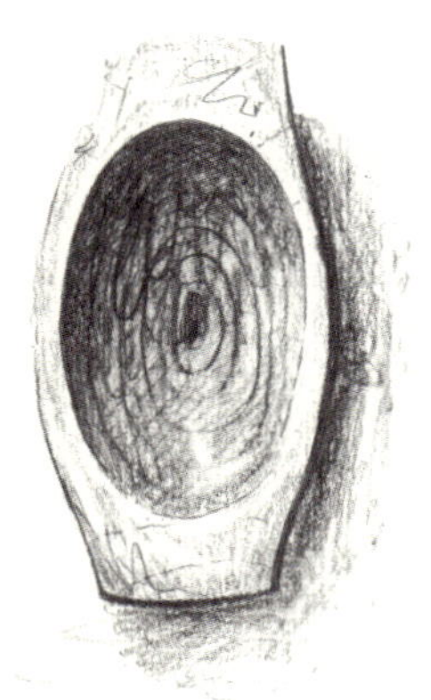

1. Rest the axe edge across the pith and strike the top with the club to split the wood into two. Using the relief cut (see page 46), carve a thin amount of wood from the cleft surface to remove any remnants of the pith from the billet. Using the same technique, axe away the bark surface, following the natural curvature of the log.

2. With the chest lever and the pull grip (see pages 53 and 52), smooth out the top saddle surface with long clean shavings. This will be our 'face' side.

Bark up or down?

Carving pith side up tends to be more favoured for larger-scale bowls as the rim is already established by the split and the belly of the bowl is already rounded. However, orienting a bowl this way increases the chances of it splitting as it dries because of the orientation of the growth rings.

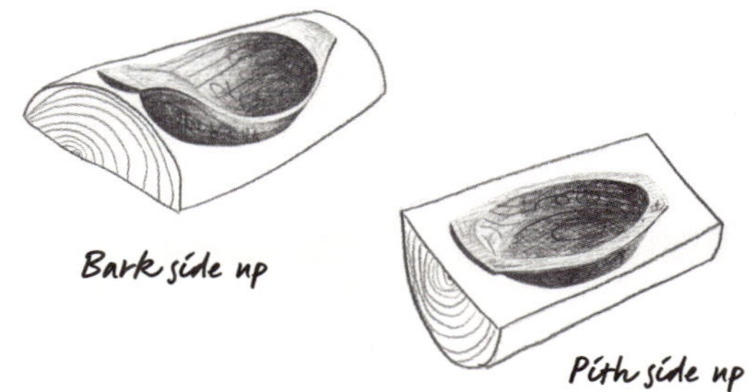

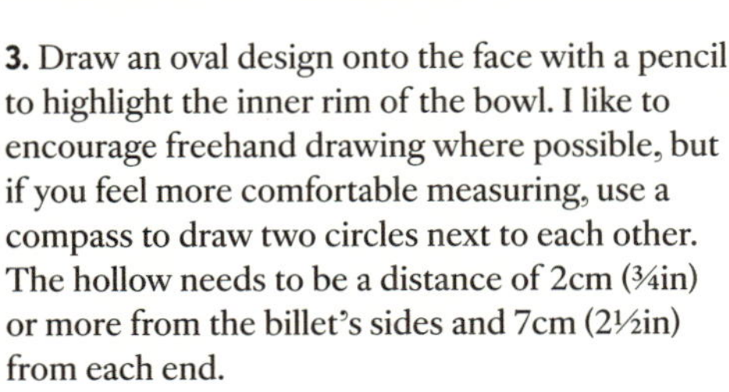

3. Draw an oval design onto the face with a pencil to highlight the inner rim of the bowl. I like to encourage freehand drawing where possible, but if you feel more comfortable measuring, use a compass to draw two circles next to each other. The hollow needs to be a distance of 2cm (¾in) or more from the billet's sides and 7cm (2½in) from each end.

4. With a saw, cut directly across the grain of the top face, through the middle of the pebble shape. Stop just shy of the pencil line. Repeat the process on both sides of the saw incision to divide the oval into four.

5.Axe out the four parts by carefully carving into the middle from each end of the pebble shape. The pre-sawn stop cuts should make axing into the middle of the valley fairly straightforward with the wood splitting out as the axe opens the fibres.

6. Once it has been roughed out, begin to hollow with the hook knife. Working across the grain with the apple peeler grip (see page 55), create a concave shape that dips beneath the edge of the rim. Start in the middle of the bowl and work outwards, turning the rough axe marks into a smooth knife finish.

Once you get the hang of hollowing, it can be easy to get carried away slightly and hollow through the bowl completely.

7. With hook knives that have a rather curved tip, you can use another technique. Hold the hook knife out in front of you with the hook pointed downwards in a clenched fist, cutting edge facing away. Rest the bowl on a flat surface and from each edge of the hollow carve into the middle, flicking the blade out with your wrist to engage the bevel into the wood. Be wary of your non-dominant hand that needs to be behind the knife at all times. Monitor the thickness as you carve with your finger and thumb, to recognize any early signs of thinning.

8. Now draw on an outer rim design that flows into a handle on both ends. A thin rim will give a more elegant feel to the bowl whereas a thicker lip will have more of a rustic charm. Begin to sculpt the exterior shape using the axe. On the sides of the billet, start from the widest part of the drawing and use the relief cut to sculpt the drawn shape towards the end of the handles.

9. On the bottom of the bowl, mark out a foot with a smaller pebble in the centre. With the axe, carve away the side profile on the edges from both sides of the foot drawing, bringing the underside into a slight ridge towards both ends of the billet. Next, axe each ridge away to the end grain, leaving behind enough material on each end to form the handle. The blank is now ready for the knife.

10. Follow the same pattern with the knife as the axe, from the foot to the ends of the handles. Begin with the chest lever grip to refine the axe marks. Use the hook knife to remove a shallow hollow from within the foot, followed by the chest lever grip with the knife to level the bumpy surface. This helps the bowl sit flat. To carve the side grain under the bowl, work across the grain with the apple peeler grip to meet the outer lip.

11. Spend some time using the thumb push grip (see page 54), cleaning up areas that seem to be raised or rough. Use the pull-cut saw to trim the two handles and tidy with the chest lever grip. To finish, chamfer the edges of the handles and both the inside and outside of the rim carefully with the apple peeler grip.

Spoon carving

Wooden spoons have stirred the pots of our culinary history for thousands of years. A three-dimensional, ergonomic object of function and design, intertwined in our everyday lives, it was the ever-growing craft of spoon carving that really got me fixed on green woodworking. I was drawn to the versatility of such a simple object and the way the playful marriage of the bowl and handle can really lend itself to a billet of wood.

Radial spoons

Radial spoons are made from one of many split billets from a single log, minimizing waste wood to carve a lot of spoons efficiently. They are usually flat and incorporate the grain that runs through the spoon like the strings of a guitar, making them strong and reliable both to carve and use.

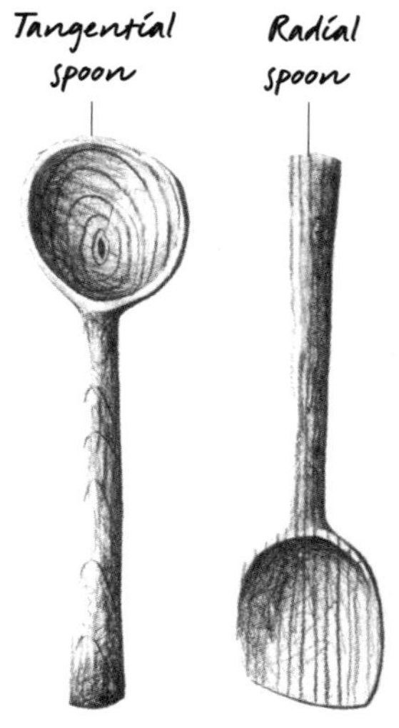

Tangential spoons

These are orientated in from the outer bark surface, burrowing into the round of branches or trunks, revealing interesting patterns. They offer more room for ergonomic features such as an upward tilted bowl tip known as a 'crank'. This orientation tends to be favoured by many spoon carvers due to the unique pattern revealed as the knife carves into the growth rings. They can also flow with curved, crooked branches known as crooks, meaning the maker can work quite sensitively, incorporating the shape within the wood's directional changes and rhythm. This can often enhance their natural aesthetics and ergonomics, while adding strength by including the grain through the length of the spoon.

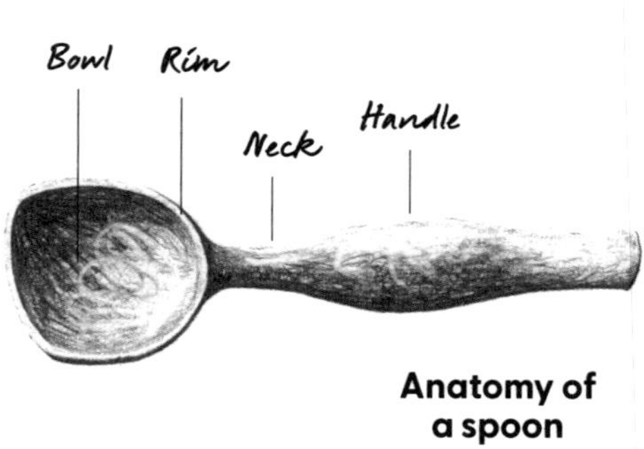

Anatomy of a spoon

Cooking spoon and eating spoon

The techniques to carve a simple radial cooking spoon (shown above in the picture opposite) are explained first, followed by instructions on how to make the more advanced tangential eating spoon. I would recommend carving a couple of radial cooking spoons before taking to the more advanced techniques. From one log of 16cm (6in) or so in diameter, up to eight radial spoons can be made. I tend to work in small batches to create a series of playful blanks of different designs to then sit and carve, slowly improving my skills as I move onto the next. A tangential spoon usually grants the opportunity to make two spoons from one branch section.

Toolkit and materials

For both types
• An axe and club, pencil, ruler (optional), hook knife and sharp carving knife.

For the cooking spoon (radial)
• Round of fresh wood at roughly 16cm (6in) or over in diameter and 30cm (12in) in length (makes up to eight spoons).

For the eating spoon (tangential)
• Branch or trunk with a minimum of 10cm (4in) in diameter and a length of about 20cm (8in).

How to make a cooking spoon

1. Resting the axe edge across the pith, split the log open into two halves. Choose the half that appears to be the straightest and split again, and again once more until you have a straight billet from one-eighth of the round. Remove the bark. Sometimes it can peel off by hand but if not, use the axe and the relief cut (see page 46) to carve the bark surface to meet the wood, remembering to work halfway down the billet at a time.

2. Repeat the relief cut on the sharp pith edge – note that when working the axe into a point, the axe will bite the wood with a lot more ease than a wider bark surface. Manoeuvre the axe gently, removing just a sliver that leaves a facet 1cm (3⁄8in) in width. This leaves two face surfaces. Choose the one that appears to be less gnarly and most free from knots or changes in grain direction, or, if they are similar, choose the widest surface.

3. If needed, you can use the axe to flatten the surface, creating a smooth canvas to draw on a design. On the face side, draw a centreline that follows the grain through the billet's length with a pencil and draw on a spoon design (see opposite for design tips).

Spoon-carving design tips

I encourage freehand drawing when it comes to designing a spoon as I find it wonderfully expressive and playful. Below are some design tips that I like to share to help with the making, usability and longevity of the piece.

Begin with the shape of the bowl as it will likely affect the rest of the composition. If you are stuck for inspiration, look around your environment and natural surroundings. Still stuck? Think about the things you enjoy cooking the most. Long spoons are suited particularly well to cooking mushy foods such as porridge, curry or risotto. Does your most-used pan have a sharp angle that will benefit from a spoon with a pointed tip to reach into the corners?

When drawing on the bowl, place it in the middle of the centreline and leave 5mm (¼in) from the top in case the wood dries out slightly on the end grain and reveals a crack.

If this is your first spoon, keep the handle simple at a consistent 2cm (¾in) thickness. Have it flow with the centreline in the middle to meet the bowl so that the whole shape has a strong grain structure running through it. If the handle naturally bows with the grain, embrace the wood's decision to meander. Avoid snaking handles that may deviate from the grain direction. Although these may be visually striking, it is a recipe for a frustrating learning process between grain direction and patience. If you want your handle to be shorter than the billet, shorten it later in the process as the length will be useful to grip while carving.

If you are new to spoon carving, make the transition from bowl to handle smooth and not too steep. If you are connecting the handle to the bowl rather harshly, soften the taper so it flows with the shape. Lastly, try not to get too precious or obsessive with your design. You'll find that it may well change and develop organically.

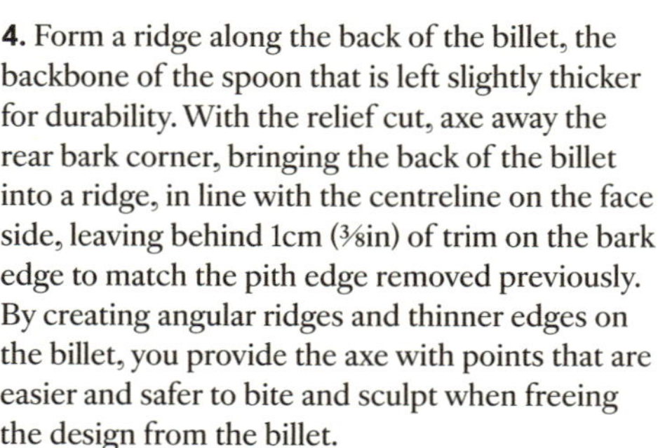

4. Form a ridge along the back of the billet, the backbone of the spoon that is left slightly thicker for durability. With the relief cut, axe away the rear bark corner, bringing the back of the billet into a ridge, in line with the centreline on the face side, leaving behind 1cm (⅜in) of trim on the bark edge to match the pith edge removed previously. By creating angular ridges and thinner edges on the billet, you provide the axe with points that are easier and safer to bite and sculpt when freeing the design from the billet.

5. Next, while still using the relief cut, narrow the two sides of the billet to meet the edges of the bowl drawing on the face side, preserving the material above the bowl for now.

I have observed the way in which new green woodcarvers work with great emotion, sensitivity and peace to reveal a spoon from a piece of locally felled wood.

6. Establish a taper from the edge of the bowl drawing to the bottom of the handle. Holding the billet by the bowl end with the handle directed into the axe block, slowly begin to break up the fibres at the bottom of the billet using the relief cut. As you begin to work up the side to meet the bowl's edge, adjust the pressure and weight of the incision to make tiny little taps as the axe rises, shortening the distance between the incisions so that the axe head doesn't lift any higher than the hand holding the billet (this protects it). It will likely take a few passes with the axe to remove the material to accurately meet the handle design.

7. With a pencil, draw two lines on the face: two-thirds into the bowl from the top of the spoon, and in the middle of the transition where the bowl meets the handle to form a cross shape. Flow these two lines around to the back of the billet. In between them will be a 'no-axing zone'. Keep the weight intact here, and taper away to sculpt out a nice back profile of your spoon while leaving behind what is known as a 'keel' of the spoon: the thicker section of the back profile that adds strength to the spoon when it is in use.

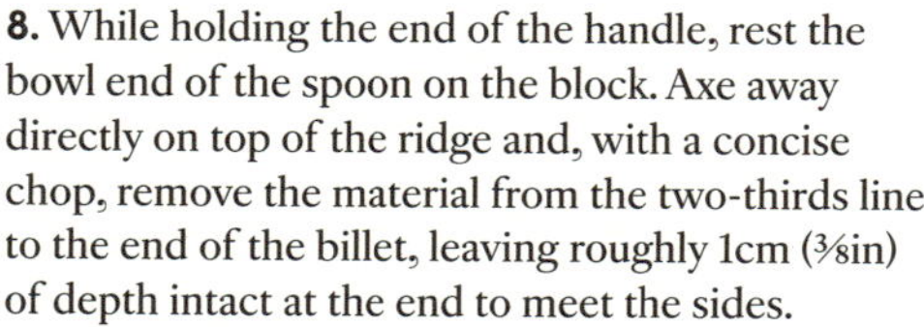

8. While holding the end of the handle, rest the bowl end of the spoon on the block. Axe away directly on top of the ridge and, with a concise chop, remove the material from the two-thirds line to the end of the billet, leaving roughly 1cm (⅜in) of depth intact at the end to meet the sides.

9. Next, rotate the spoon to hold the bowl. With the relief cut, develop a gradual taper from the transition line, towards the end of the back of the handle. I recommend first removing a thin sliver of material to then play with the spoon to see how it feels in the hand, and remove more if required.

10. To round the top of the bowl, hold the spoon, facing outwards by the end of the handle in your non-dominant hand, with the bowl end placed in the middle of the axe block. Stand over the top of the spoon, sighting down onto the face side and begin to take off a small sliver of material from the corner of the spoon bowl. Gently drop your non-dominant hand away from the axe as it repeats its motion, creating an arc with the handle – gradually removing wood as you go to bring the cut into the centreline. Spin the spoon around, so that it is now facing towards you, and repeat, taking a slight step back to view the spoon, bringing the cut into a point to meet the other in the centre. Work the material on each side, reducing the point gradually until it is nicely rounded to meet the line.

11. Before moving onto the knife work, spend some time with your blank and recognize areas that you think you will be able to remove with the axe. How close can you get to your pencil line? The more the billet is reduced at this stage, the more refined the overall outcome will be.

12. The bowl can now be hollowed with the hook knife, using the apple peeler grip (see page 55). Hold the spoon across the body with its handle in line with the handle of the hook knife. With your thumb placed safely beneath the rim, work across the grain within a small penny size circumference, aiming to remove a small, wafer thin shaving to begin.

13. Once the hollow is established, begin to open it out gradually, focusing on the width, not depth: enter the tool earlier and depart the tool later, exaggerating slightly the articulation of the hand as it closes with a controlled flick of the wrist. Once you have met the shallow hollow to the edges of your pencil line, work in a continuous sweep with the hook knife from edge to edge to establish your overall depth.

Hollowing tips

Deep hollows on cooking spoons encourage the food to clog when in use and tend to be more suited for serving spoons, ladles or scoops. Shallower hollows are much more practical for pushing and stirring. Before you start hollowing, draw a small perimeter around the outside of the bowl to determine how thick you want the rim to be. A thin edge around the bowl will give an elegant feel to the spoon while a thicker rim will offer a more rustic charm. The pencil-drawn cross through the bowl (see step 7) highlights the deepest part of a spoon bowl and the starting point for the hollow.

14. To remove the cleft surface from the top face of the bowl, use the chest lever grip (see page 53) with the straight knife to bring the lip flat.

15. Once the bowl is nicely hollowed, refine the rest of the spoon's shape with the straight knife. The grain on the back runs in two directions, as defined by the axe earlier. Use the chest lever grip to sculpt the material from the top of the keel to the end of the bowl to form a multi-faceted, convex underside.

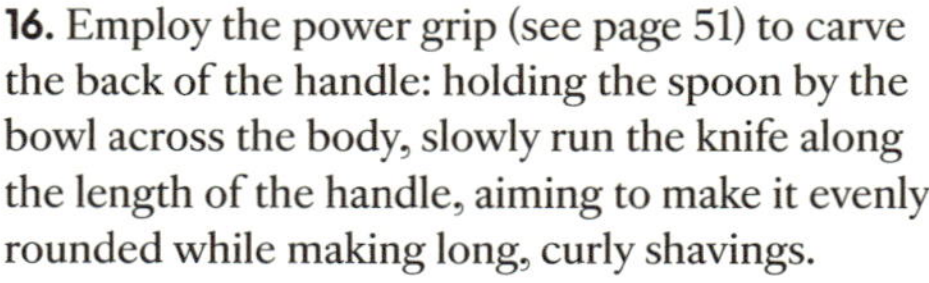

16. Employ the power grip (see page 51) to carve the back of the handle: holding the spoon by the bowl across the body, slowly run the knife along the length of the handle, aiming to make it evenly rounded while making long, curly shavings.

17. Now use the squeezy nature of the apple peeler grip to efficiently blend the back of the bowl into the neck. Hold the spoon upright on your lap in your non-dominant hand, making good use of the handle's length. In the other hand, place the thumb on one side of the spoon's neck and the knife on the other side in the clutch of the hand. Gently close your hand to take away some material on the sharp edge where the back of the bowl meets the handle. The spoon's neck will protect your thumb from intercepting the knife. You can also use the apple peeler grip and the thumb push grip (see page 54) to smooth the rough texture around the bowl's perimeter, observing the grain direction to work towards each end grain of the bowl.

If you find the knife is catching in particular areas, the grain may want to be worked in the other direction.

18. Using the pull grip (see page 52), carve the top surface and the sides of the spoon handle. Holding the spoon bowl into the chest, draw the knife back along the sharp corner of the flat face, keeping the knife consistent against the wood when the bevel is engaged. Rotate the spoon in your sternum to expose new points of the handle to the knife while keeping the blade articulation repetitive and consistent. Twist the spoon around, this time holding by the spoon bowl, with the handle braced into the sternum, and draw the knife back again to meet the untidy parts with a nice finish. In this direction, you can sculpt the pockets in the neck transition, blending the bowl into the handle. The end of the handle can be finished easily with the thumb push grip, or sawn to your preferred length.

19. Spend some time refining the overall shape. Once you are happy with the overall shape of the spoon, use a combination of both the apple peeler and the thumb push grip to chamfer the edges on the end of the handle and around the outside of the bowl, making them less sharp, adding longevity to the spoon.

Thoughts on

Developing a style

Each individual woodcarver will practise in their own, unique way. The woodcarving world blossoms with personality, quirks and shapes that continue to push the craft to new levels of ingenuity. I believe everyone has a style that can evolve naturally as skills develop.

A style should not be forced nor squeezed into a box, but should be listened to and nourished. A personal style is a creative identity that encompasses natural responses like emotion, inspiration and techniques.

When I began carving, I was drawn to the process of refinement. I would often feel as though I was being too much of a perfectionist when trying to make a piece extremely smooth and rounded. Just by running my fingertips along the facets, I could notice a piece of wood that didn't need to be there. Instead of feeling discouraged by it, I began to understand it more and embrace it as an ability to be meticulous. I set out to carve the smoothest cup that I could possibly make to satisfy it. I am now known for making these refined pieces and I recognize this as my style, which has evolved organically over the years.

I like to think that a style can really bloom simply by creating things that bring you the most joy. Stay curious and begin to understand your relationship with craft. Ask yourself questions as to why you are drawn to particular techniques, processes or shapes when making.

How to make an eating spoon

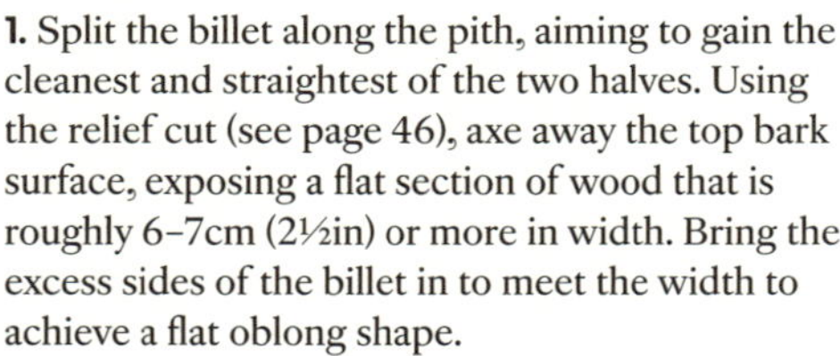

1. Split the billet along the pith, aiming to gain the cleanest and straightest of the two halves. Using the relief cut (see page 46), axe away the top bark surface, exposing a flat section of wood that is roughly 6–7cm (2½in) or more in width. Bring the excess sides of the billet in to meet the width to achieve a flat oblong shape.

2. With a pencil, draw a line across the grain at roughly two thirds towards one end of the billet. This highlights where you begin to form what is known as the 'crank' in an eating spoon. The valley to form the crank is instigated by a stop cut – an incision into the grain that stops the fibres in their tracks, to be met with a shaving from either side to form a valley into the straight billet. Start by creating an incision or 'notch' straight across the fibres of the bowl on the line drawn through it. There are two methods of creating the notch. The easiest method is to use a pull-cut saw, cutting to a depth of 1.5cm (½in) or so. Secondly, opt for axing straight across the fibres onto the line, keeping your non-dominant hand far away, grasping at the very end of the billet, away from the line of the axe.

3. The notch highlights the deepest part of the spoon bowl's profile. Before widening the notch to create a valley, draw onto the billet two lines to visualize the form of an eating spoon's bowl. A gradual slope joins the tip of the billet to the bottom of the notch, while a steeper kick flicks up to highlight the back of the bowl. The overall shape reminds me of a tick, which suggests a rough silhouette of an eating spoon.

4. Next you can use the axe to remove material from either side of the notch to establish the tick shape. Firstly, work from the back of the bowl, into the notch, holding the spoon in your non-dominant hand by the longer section. Work the wood in thin slivers, removing a controlled amount at a time. Be careful not to follow through with the axe, resulting in splitting out the opposing material.

Designing a crank

A crank is the ergonomic upward pointed angle of the bowl that encourages the tip to sit above the line of the handle when the spoon is in use. It is formed by making a valley in the bowl area of the blank to achieve the correct angle and three-dimensional rough profile, before shaping the two-dimensional outline of the spoon.

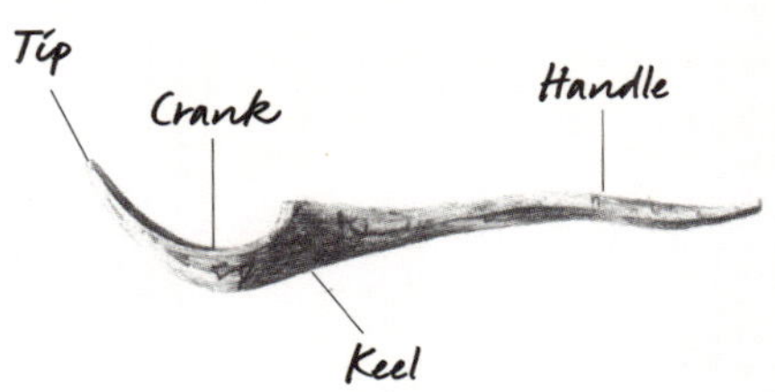

5. When taking material away from the tip of the bowl into the notch, there isn't a handle to hold. Use a different approach by reclining the spoon onto the block to support it from behind safely. Rest the billet on its side, exposing the top of the thick end towards you and your axe, aligning the bottom of the notch with the edge of the axe block. Support the billet by clasping your non-dominant hand on the end of the handle, creating an arc with your elbow, resting your forearm on the block itself. Lower your stance so the direction of the axe when swung will now hit horizontally into the edge of the axe block. The aim here is to have the axe's follow-through controlled by the interception of the axe block so that it doesn't travel farther than needed. To cut, the billet itself intercepts the axe from the top of the billet at the required angle to meet the bottom of the notch while protecting your non-dominant arm. Sight the axe from the top. This technique is to be practised slowly, especially for the first few cranks.

6. Once the crank is established, revert back to the relief cut to remove a fraction of material from the top of the handle, working away from the bowl to have it sit lower than the tip of the spoon for enhanced ergonomics.

7. Draw the spoon design onto the cranked face of the wood following a centreline.

8. The billet can now be treated in a similar way as the cooking spoon to form a blank. Narrow the billet to meet your bowl drawing and create a taper from the edge of the bowl towards the end of the handle. A stop cut can also be made on any part of the spoon where the shape changes direction quickly.

9. Hold the spoon billet by the tip of the bowl, resting on its side towards the neck of the spoon on the edge of the axe block, handle angled downwards towards the ground. With an axe or pull-cut saw, create a notch in the side of the billet at the base of the bowl to meet the pencil drawing. Repeat on the other side.

It is when making these careful, refining cuts that I recognize the carving axe as a tool for gentle sculpting and shaping.

10. Remove the waste material on both sides of the handle by pinching the end of the billet and carefully axing away the fibres towards the notch, beneath the fingertips. When working towards the bowl, take care not to accidentally split the necessary material away. By carefully repeating the stroke of the axe at the same incision, and levering the axe head to the side slightly, try to pry the fibres apart towards the stop cut, preventing the need for the axe to follow through and take out half of the bowl.

11. Once the sides of the handle have been removed, axe the back profile, taking material from the sharp edges first to form a ridge along the back of the handle. Then axe directly onto the spine away from the bowl to sculpt the back profile while leaving some mass on the neck to establish a strong keel.

12. Finally, with the axe, round the top of the spoon bowl and add a suitable convex to the underside, rounding the back of the bowl to form a rim.

13. Although the rest of the spoon can be made using the same methods as the cooking spoon (from step 12 on page 126), the following advanced grip will come in rather useful for the fussier angles of an eating spoon. The grip stems from the pull grip (see page 52): bringing the spoon into the sternum while clasping the end of the blank with your fingers. Pinch the end of the spoon with your index finger and thumb to free up your remaining three fingers. These fingers can then guide the spine of the knife for increased strength and command of the pivot. This grip adds higher levels of control in tricky areas such as where the bowl meets the neck, the top lip of the bowl and the top saddle of the handle.

Thoughts on

Woodcarving communities

The green woodcarving universe has grown astronomically since I began carving. The increase in popularity was initially described as a heritage craft resurgence when some makers reintroduced pre-industrial revolution, almost forgotten crafts to others in the form of teaching and awareness spreading through articles and blogs. The community is now recognized as an expansive culture, a movement of like-minded folk who practise making, share skills and ultimately live a slower pace of life.

From makers young, old, new and experienced, there is such warmth and beauty in craft folk. I felt instantly welcomed when I first stepped foot into a spoon-carving club. It was the first time putting myself out there after being diagnosed with depression – while I lacked confidence in the beginning, I feel like now I have gained a family that accepts me and gives me huge purpose.

Our community is spread across the world, connected by international carving festivals, courses, meet-ups, Internet groups and social media. Though we may not see each other for extended periods of time, makers are deeply connected to one another by their exchange of crafts and carvings.

Today, you are never too far away from a carving club or course. Though they may still be a little niche and may not be as easy to find as other clubs, I tend to find that asking around or embarking on an Internet search generally reveals other makers who are excited to share their skills and knowledge. I believe the rise of woodcarvers is linked to the lack of tactility and the amount of technology within our busy daily lives. I hope that green woodcarving continues to grow and be shared as a healthy, holistic, expressive art form.

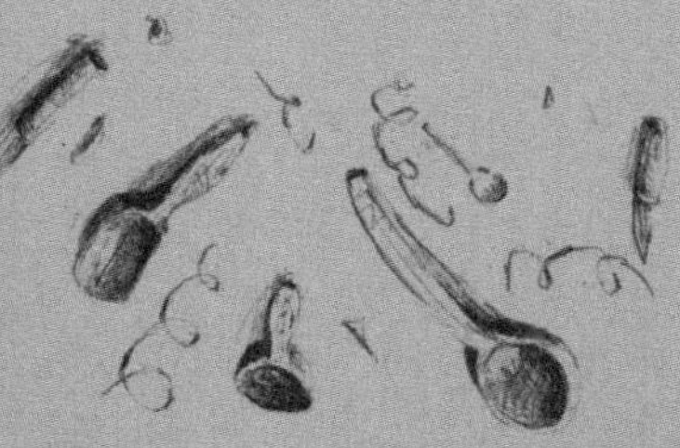

Finishing, decoration and aftercare

Not only is there a great deal of escapism in green woodcarving but there are also many opportunities to showcase your creativity and attention to detail in finishing and decorating pieces. When revisiting a carving after it is dry, you may decide it needs something extra to enhance it. This could be a little pop of colour or a chip-carved pattern. Perhaps it may need nothing at all – just applying a simple coat of oil is often enough.

After carving

Once carved, a piece may still need to be nurtured to ensure that it can withstand the rigours of everyday use. After taking a step back, sometimes your work still continues to speak to you and you may wish to change and evolve it. These flutters of inspiration can occur even after you thought you had finished.

Drying your carvings

After carving, the water in between the wood fibres needs to evaporate. If the drying process in green wood happens too quickly, the piece will likely crack, heartbreakingly undoing all of your hard efforts. Collect some of the wood chips that it was made with and wrap them, together along with the piece, into a bag or cloth made from a natural, breathable material such as a paper bag or tote bag.

Put the bundle into a cool, dark place in the home or shed, away from a heating source or draft. Places like the cupboard under the sink or a shelf in the basement work really well to draw the moisture into the atmosphere slowly. Most projects will take a week or so to season – after this, they will be touch dry, make a brittle acoustic sound and will be much lighter than before. You may notice that the piece is slightly smaller – perhaps it is oxidized and is now darker in colour or maybe it has twisted or warped – these are just reminders of wood's beautiful unpredictability.

Finishing cuts and burnishing

Once dry, a piece may reveal untidy areas where the knife may not have connected well with the wood. In some woods the fibres may have raised slightly where the moisture escaped. Running the knife edge along the top surface and re-carving some areas may be necessary to re-establish a smooth finish. The tip of the knife is agile and nimble and can be used to refine tight curves and transitions.

Burnishing is another technique that smooths the surface of the wood by flattening the raised fibres. It is performed by rubbing the spine of a knife or a smooth pebble/marble lightly on the wood repeatedly until shiny.

Chip carving

Regarded by many practising makers as its very own artform, chip carving is the removal of wood in an ornate, decorative style with a series of notch-like cuts. High-level, expert chip carving would need its very own book or series of courses to tutor and master but the fundamentals can be relatively easy to pick up. Simple Scandinavian triangle-style chip carving requires three incisions with the tip of the knife, employing the thumb push grip and the apple peeler grip (see pages 54 and 55) to make simple, folksy geometric-style patterns.

First, draw a small triangle guide onto the designated area of your piece. With the thumb push grip, stab two incisions directly into two of the lines, perpendicular to the face at a 90-degree angle. Meet the two incisions with an apple peeler squeeze cut with the tip of the knife into the point of the triangle at a shallow angle, about 30 degrees to the wood, to pop off and relieve a chip. The triangle can be repeated like a stamp to form rhythmic patterns on handles and surfaces.

Kolrosing

This is a decorative Scandinavian style of pattern making in wood. The knife is used like a pencil to tattoo illustrative drawings into the surface. Like an etching, the knife's tip can be scribed into the surface to pry the wood apart. A fine staining powder such as ground coffee, cinnamon or even coal dust is then lightly rubbed into the surface with your fingertips. It doesn't need to be worked too hard into the wood, just enough to sit into the open crevices left behind by the knife. Wipe or sand away any excess and seal it with a suitable oil. For more control when mark making, a scalpel may be better suited for this than a carving knife. Some bladesmiths even make knives specifically for kolrosing.

Colour and tone

It is incredible how adding a splash of colour can really enhance your carving and the playfulness of your creations. Wood often has its own hidden and unique tonal qualities that can be unleashed with a little knowledge, adding a deeper level of understanding between the maker and the material.

Painting and staining wood

Like a canvas, your pieces can be painted with gouache, acrylic and oil-based paints found in the home. For pieces that may come into contact with food, I find milk paint to be a safe option that is readily available in many colours and quantities online. Milk paint is essentially powdered pigment and milk proteins that, when hydrated, bond to wood robustly. It dries to a matte finish that can be enhanced with oil, sanded back slightly to reveal the facets of the wood or can be layered to create interesting colour combinations.

Experimenting with homemade paints and stains is a huge creative journey in itself. Colours can be made from simple household ingredients such as tea, coffee, beetroot, cinnamon and turmeric, all mixed with a little water and painted directly onto the wood. Deeper colours can be achieved by boiling black walnut husks or acorns in water and leaving overnight. The tannins in the husks are released, darkening the water to make a stain. Some makers even cook their treen to successfully bake a deeper tone into the wood. Oil lightly with a rag before baking in the middle of the oven for 30 minutes at 180°C (350°F), while attentively keeping an eye on it and oiling again after.

Oiling

Oiling your work not only deepens the tone and enhances the patterns of wood, but it also creates a barrier that seals and protects exposed grain from wear, tear and bacteria.

There are four oils I like to recommend to finish your pieces: walnut oil, tung nut oil, raw linseed oil and hemp seed oil. These four oils are organic, food safe and, unlike other oil types commonly found in the house, they polymerize – cure and harden into a solid state to shield the material. Your olive oil in the cupboard, used for cooking, will always stay in a fluid state and, over time, will begin to rot and go rancid when between wood fibres.

Though some makers choose to soak their treen in baths of oil, most projects only require a generous massage of oil into the wood with clean hands or a rag, then leaving in a sunny spot to polymerize for a few days before using. Note that when using linseed oil it can spontaneously combust if left exposed on a cloth. Oiling is a magical closing step – you'll be able to see the wood darken slightly and come to life: facets will gleam and dance in the light and the grain will reveal all of its hidden mysteries.

Ebonizing

Tannins are naturally occurring compounds sometimes found in specific woods, barks, plants, galls and fruits. When present in wood, they react with a solution called iron acetate, which can create a dye when brushed on the wood's surface, dramatically and permanently darkening the colour. This food-safe process is called ebonizing and was traditionally used on common tannin-heavy woods to give the illusion of being made from darker, more expensive woods like ebony and sold for higher prices. It has since been used to creatively enhance wood carving projects by giving them a darker and more artistic feel. Hardwoods that are naturally high in tannins and perfect for ebonizing include walnut, oak, chestnut and cherry. Iron acetate can be made easily at home by placing steel wool into a clean glass jar with some vinegar.

Making the ebonizing solution

1. Wash the steel wool with some hot water and soap to remove any unwanted oils from the manufacturing process. Wearing gloves, place it into a jar and pour over enough white cleaning vinegar to cover it.

2. Seal the jar with plastic wrap and poke a hole in the top so the gases can escape. Place the jar outside or in a shed for a week, disturbing it slightly each day to encourage the vinegar to cover the wool. The vinegar will gradually dissolve the wool leaving behind the iron acetate solution.

3. After a week, open the jar and filter the solution three times through an old cloth or coffee filter and seal in a clean glass jar until you are ready to use it.

4. Apply to dry wood by brushing it on and watch the magic happen. The wood will immediately begin to turn black with the chemical reaction. To achieve a darker tone, the piece can be first brushed with a damp tea bag to create higher tannin levels before the solution is applied.

5. Dry the piece again for at least a week and polish the surface with a clean rag before use or oiling.

Caring for wood

Over time, your carved creations will display signs of wear, especially those exposed to food, heat and frequent washing. When washing woodenware, use mild soaps if any at all with warm water and dry them upside down, away from direct sunlight, being careful not to encourage pools of water or fast drying. While the patina of life left behind on a handmade object is beautiful, sometimes wood will need some loving care. When they need oiling, your carvings will feel dry and appear paler than before. A fluffy spoon that has stirred a thousand pots may need the top surface re-carved. A crack in a bowl can be stitched with some copper wire to ensure it doesn't continue its path and a butter spreader's edge can be re-established to live and sweep another slice of toast.

A life lived with woodcraft means you will always have the indulgence of being able to 'make another one'.

Glossary

bark: a tree's armour.

bevel: the material removed to form the sharp edge of a blade.

billet: a piece of wood, split from a round.

bite point: the contact point of the edge of the knife into the material.

blank: a crude, axed-out, rough version of an object for carving.

burr: a minuscule, often hair-like amount of metal brushed towards an edge of a tool during its sharpening process.

cambium: cells between the wood and the bark that produce new bark or new wood.

chamfer: often a 45-degree removal of material that intercepts a sharp 90-degree edge.

chattering marks: an untidy finish where the contact between edge and wood was not correct.

crank: the ergonomic angle between a spoon bowl and handle.

end grain: the end of a piece of wood where fibres stop.

facet: the negative space left behind by carving away wood.

grain: the alignment of wood fibres that make up a tree's structure.

green wood: Freshly felled, unseasoned timber with a high moisture content.

hardwood: woods from broadleaf trees.

heartwood: the more compact, inner part of a log.

medullary: patterns of shimmering rays caused by the cellular structure of wood.

pith: the central stem of a tree.

rive/riving: calculative splitting of wood, often in longer lengths.

sapwood: younger, softer rows of wood.

softwood: from trees that commonly make needles or cones.

spalting: patterns (often dramatic) in wood caused by fungus.

spine: the back of a blade.

stop cut: where a longer shaving-like cut meets a harsher incision- like notch to create quick direction changes in forms.

tannin: a chemical found in wood, fruits and nuts.

tear out: when fibres break or splinter away.

treen: wooden objects, usually made from one piece of wood.

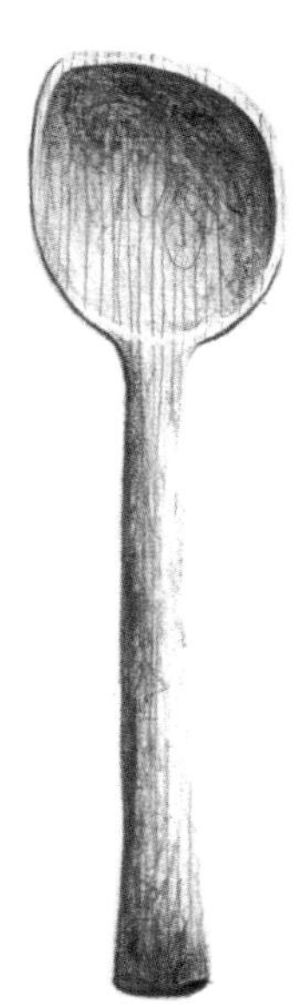

Index

A short goodbye

The opportunity to write this book enabled me to reflect deeply on my practice as a whole and re-walk the path of my career for the first time. What began as a storm has now watered a forest that continues to grow wildly. After spending dark periods of my life feeling hopeless, I am forever grateful to woodcarving for showing me light. To share my knowledge while keeping my creative intensity burning to inspire others fills me with joy. I really wouldn't have thought I could ever reach a point on this journey to be able to give back to the craft in this capacity.

Although a life full of craft seems romantic, making a living from it is tough. For a long time I would always separate what I did for a living with what I did for life. A lot of makers have part-time jobs around the clock to not only keep themselves afloat, but to also support their craft. My healthy relationship with craft stems from previously working a day job and indulging myself with carving in my spare time. I put less financial pressure on carving because I knew it was volatile and didn't want to ever feel discouraged by it. I have always strived to maintain a mindset to make, primarily for the sake of making.

It is my hope that this craft continues to flourish to a point where it will become deservedly recognized as a form of mindful therapy and for the sophisticated art that it is. I hope this book encourages you to notice, learn from and support green woodworking.

My connection with craft and education is an endless river that flows as I continue to be inspired and develop my skills with new techniques. In the strange and loud world we live in, I hope you find stillness and take a lot away from this introduction and unravel your own relationship with green woodcarving. Once you no longer require this book, I would be grateful if you could pass it on to someone who may also benefit from it, to expand the ripple. If you wish to share your creations, I would be delighted to see them. Please don't hesitate to contact me via my website, www.samuelalexandershapes.com.

Samuel Alexander

About the author

Samuel Alexander first started whittling as a way to help him recover from depression, discovering that it not only lifted his mood but also yielded beautiful keepsakes like spoons, bowls and ornaments. Soon he was selling what he made, and became one of TOAST's New Makers of 2022. He has taught whittling and green woodcarving at workshops across the UK and his compelling, calming Instagram videos have attracted a new generation of followers and carvers. Now based in the Czech Republic, this is his first book on the subject.

www.samuelalexandershapes.com
Instagram: @samuelalexandershapes

Acknowledgements

I would like to acknowledge Skittledog and Thames & Hudson for this opportunity and for making the visual arts accessible to all. Thank you especially to Zara Larcombe for recognizing me and my commitment to spread the healing word of woodcraft. I would also like to thank Virginia Brehaut for her energy and coordination – together with talented photographer Charles Emerson, we were able to add so much heart to this project. Thank you also to the vision of Masumi Briozzo and Felicity Awdry for their design and production.

I feel blessed to have stepped foot into Wilderness Woods in East Sussex to capture the images for this book (wildernesswood.org) and share the oasis that is their woodland. I have never experienced a woodland so full of life, where togetherness and laughter blow through the trees along with the birdsong. Thank you to Emily for letting us photograph there and to the skilled craftspeople that built the cabins. They have demonstrated what it can be like to live your life in a sanctuary surrounded by both nature and craft.

In my home sanctuary, I would like to express my appreciation and gratitude to my wife Kateřina for her endless encouragement, love and patience that kept me grounded and created a space for me to give the best that I could to this book. To my beautiful daughter who began life as a little seedling at the start of the manuscript, and beamed at me like the sun with so much life through the duration of the project. Watching you grow is infinitely inspirational. I am grateful to my family here in Czechia and my sister Emilie in the UK for their support; along with dear friends Cecilie, Cyriaque and Ed for their honesty and wisdom.

I would like to thank the green woodworking community for its generosity, shelter and warm friendship, especially to all the members of London Greenwood (londongreenwood.com) for cooperatively providing a space for folk like me to have affordable access to green woodwork. To all the participants who I have taught and to toolmakers Nic Westermann, Adrian Lloyd, Svante Djarv, James Wood, Mora, Tormek and Silky Saws. Lastly, thank you to you, and to the trees that continue to inspire me.

For Nora

First published in the United Kingdom in 2025 by Skittledog,
an imprint of Thames & Hudson Ltd, 181A High Holborn,
London WC1V 7QX

Senior Editor: Virginia Brehaut
Cover Designer: Alison Guile
Designer: Masumi Briozzo
Production: Felicity Awdry
Photographer: Charles Emerson

British Library Cataloguing-in-Publication Data
A catalogue record for this book is available from the British Library

ISBN 978-1-837-76064-0

Impression 01

Printed and bound in China by C and C Offset Printing Co., Ltd